Acknowledgements

This book would not have been possible without the support and inspiration of a lot of people. I would like to thank the people who helped me with proof reading and input on story selection. I would like to especially thank Phil Littlewood and Pam Craig. It was quite a task to put something like this together and I had quite a few moments of fear and nearly backed out. It was the tireless encouragement of Pam which prevented me from quitting. The design and creative input that Phil brought to this project made it what it is. His knowledge of the printing industry and layout is unparalleled. I could not have created this book without his help. I would also like to thank Amie Littlewood for her patience and understanding in the time away from Phil that this project required. I would also like to thank all of the people who have offered kind words and inspiration along the way.

Sincerely

Kris Patterson

Foreward

In 2005 Ike Patterson was presented with a Port Alberni Heritage Award in recognition of his constant work to raise community awareness of local heritage. Ike was hugely successful in engaging people in recognizing and preserving, and enjoying, their own history. His columns got people talking - reminiscing, arguing about how things really happened, searching out long-forgotten photographs – valuing what makes us a community, not a group of individuals. Ike really understood this community and had an amazing capacity for remembering detail. He also truly understood and appreciated the hard work carried out by volunteers on the ground in heritage preservation, whether that was Historical Society members doing the careful work required to conserve and make accessible the paper treasures in the archives, or men in coveralls nudging old trucks to life again.

I am so pleased that Kris Patterson has taken on the task of completing some of his father's work. These columns are a valuable community record. Ike was always one to remind us of a milestone that needed celebrating, so it is doubly appropriate that this book is released as part of Port Alberni's centennial celebrations. We could not celebrate historic milestones were it not for those who really care about local history, who preserve our community's records and then make heritage accessible in a way that engages the general public. Ike was one of those who really cared and he had the gift of making history engaging. This book is testament to those gifts and will be welcome reading.

Jean McIntosh
Director, Alberni Valley Museum

Introduction

What you hold in your hands is a selection of stories written by Old Ike Patterson. They appear in no set order and drawn from his That Was Then, This Is Now column in the Pennyworth along with some from TimeLine which appeared in the AV Times. Some others are drawn from Our Town as well as the Extra. Ike was a columnist from 2005 until his passing in 2011.

My Mom and Dad were very community minded people and we spent many, many hours discussing Port Alberni and the great people of this beautiful city. My dad's singular interest in history lead to countless hours of him interacting with people, old newspapers, books anything that would give him a little more information into this town. This passion and love for his community and its history was rivaled only by his love for my mom his soul mate. Ike had always planned on publishing his stories in a book and I know it was on his mind recently, however he never had the opportunity. I would like to thank everyone who helped in the creation of this book and the purchasers for allowing me the opportunity to fulfill my dads dream. I think it is rare to be given the chance to fulfill a dream and Port Alberni is the place that makes it possible. I feel like I have gotten to know my dad on a whole new level with the many hours that went into editing, compiling the stories that made up this volume. My dad always encouraged feedback from people as he said that is where the real history is. Due to space and other constraints it was not possible to include every story Ike has ever published. If there is a story that was done in the past you would like to see in a future volume please email me at ikesthiswasthen@gmail.com I will do my best to make sure it is included.

Publisher's note** Reader response to Old Ike's articles has been overwhelming, so in the next several months we will be "re-visiting" some of his previous columns from 2003 and 2004, before THIS WAS THEN started appearing as a weekly feature in the Pennyworth. They have been updated where necessary and will appear under the banner "THIS WAS THEN..AGAIN." I hope you enjoy reading them all, and at this time it is my pleasure to announce that plans are in the works for a 32-page collection. Linda Patterson Now....from February 5th, 2004....

THIS WAS THEN...AGAIN!
"Appreciate The Little Things"

Something happened at the January 31st, 2004 Bulldogs game to jog my "life lesson" memory button. Actually it was somebody that triggered the switch. An elderly gentleman re-introduced himself to me, as I took his Bulldogs' ticket. He reminded me that just over 30 years ago, during my broadcasting years at CJAV, he had won my "cowboy hat" on a contest.

Later, between periods of the game, this excited-to-find-me-still-in-town-prize-winning fan from the past, came back to the Multi-plex's main entrance, and we had a nice cha t about the good old days. He was one of hundreds of prize winners back in the 70's when on the last weekend before Labour Day, I did a show called "30 Hours of Solid Gold".

This "Summer Tradition" started in 1972, and broadcasting for 30 straight hours was a tremendous feat, because radio was "live" all the time, no automation then. There is no way I could go without sleep for 48 hours now.

This chance meeting revived many other fond memories that I'll treasure for the rest of my life, and for this column, I've taken two out of the archives vault. The first was the honour of being nominated for, then publicly elected to, the Port Alberni and Area "Community Resources Board" back in the mid 70's. Unfortunately the Board idea of giving local residents a voice in the planning and delivery of services never became a reality because of a change in provincial governments.

A much younger "old" Ike on the "Western Express" television show on November 25, 1981

Then in 1981, I found out that a local listener, the late Tom Parkinson, had sent my name in to the Western Canada Lottery Foundation to be a co-host on the "Western Express" TV show in Winnipeg. Talk about a pleasant surprise, and having someone think enough of you to make such a nice gesture.

My mother always told me things, but one that has stayed with me, besides good manners and trying your best, was to remember that good things will out weigh the bad.

Well, I can tell you it's absolutely true. I can also tell you it's nice to know the little things we do in a lifetime that sort of fade over the years in our mind, don't always dull in others.

You can touch the lives of so many people, in the span of one's existence, and it's really gratifying to realize you've left a positive, good feeling memory or two along the way.

Thanks again, see you at the next Bulldogs home game this fall.

Remember "30 Hours of Solid Gold" with hundreds of dollars in prizes and the biggest hits from the late 40's to the mid 70's? This studio photo was from August 26, 1977.

Third & Angus in the 30's

Third and Angus, Port Alberni in the late 1930's courtesy of Ike Patterson's Collection.

This month I thought we would look back at one of Port Alberni's most famous intersections, "Third & Angus." the way it was in the late 30's.

On the left, with the photographer standing in front of what is now Ralphs Mens wear, you can get a great view of the historic Post Office.

This building dominated the downtown core for decades and was featured on post cards until it's demise in the late 50's.

Rumor has it that the building was deemed unsafe and beyond repair, but more on that in a future story. Looking up Third past the Post office, you'll see GILES Meat Market and G.A.D. FLITTON'S Hardware and Home furnishings.

These two buildings were later modernized and still stand today, the home of Odgers Jewellers, CJAV and the Community Policing Station. There were no other businesses in the block at the time.

Now on the right, you see the same intersection looking down Third Avenue, as if you were standing in the middle of the street near Zellers. Notice the Beaufort Hotel, on the right of the photo?

Now look over to the Post Office, then down to where the TD Bank is today. You"ll see a small building which was ISOBEL'S LADIES WEAR, owned and operated for decades by ISOBEL & GEORGE MacWILLIAMS. REMEMBER..there are over 1500 historical photographs in the Alberni Valley Museum's Collection, dating from the late 1800's to the past few decades, so if you're researching for a report or a reunion, make an appointment to "look back" by calling 723-2181.

The Valley's First Hotel...The Alberni!!

Origin of photo unknown

Historical records of the time reveal the Sarrault family, who had a small water-driven sawmill on Kitsuksis Creek, built the Alberni probably in 1891.(a couple of years before Matt Ward built the Arlington) The hotel faced on Victoria Quay, opposite where the Somass Branch No. 169 now stands. As you can see from the photo on the left, the Alberni was a two-storey building with a double decker veranda and with three dormer windows on either side of the attic. The turn of the century saw Mr. and Mrs. Gus Labelle operating the Alberni and records show that in 1909 Harry Fitzgerald was the proprietor. It would also appear that Billy McAllister was the next owner and the final one to operate this pioneer establishment. With the railroad arriving, hopes were high for the local hotel business and McAllister had big plans for his hostelry. Then just prior to the first World War, the Alberni received a very stylish addition, which completely dwarfed the original building. The picture below shows the new Alberni, which boasted modern hot water heating, modern plumbing, handsome brass beds, a billiard parlor, and a new bar. Unfortunately, circumstances slowed business, the hotel stood empty for many years, being home to bats and young kids playing hide-and-seek, before being torn down. More on the Valley's hotels in coming weeks.

DID YOU KNOW??? What is now "Hollies Executive Golf Course" started out in 1968 as "Alpar Golf" under the proprietorship of Jack Luckhurst, a former Port Alberni mayor. In 1970, Roger Goddard and Ray Kwok took over the driving range, nine-hole par three golf course, plus equipment rentals and sales, at the site along the Alberni Highway. They started building a clubhouse in 1972, and it was finished the next year. The rest, they say, is history.

A "picture in time" from Fran Earthy's Photo Album!!

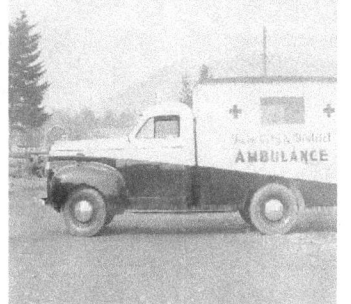

This photo from 1947, shows the new "Twin Cities & District" Ambulance, which operated out of the Alberni Fire Hall on Helen Street, at the time. Fran Earthy's late husband, Dennis, who was one of the Volunteer Fire Fighters, snapped this shot shortly after the ambulance went into service.

Photo courtesy of Vic Laughlin's family.

In this picture taken after completion of the renovations, just prior to World War 1, you can still see a portion of the original Alberni on the extreme left.

Old Business.... Go back 49 years to 1956..and re-visit some of the Valley's "forgotten" businesses. You could have shopped for Flour, Feed, Hardware and Paint at The CO-OP, at Merrifield and Johnston, where Wynans Furniture is located today. You might have had your vehicle serviced at VALLEY CAR Automotive Repairs on Tenth Avenue North. MARTIN'S CAFE, on Argyle half a block down from Third Avenue advertised "everything to satisfy your appetite" including "chicken in the straw." On my first visit to Port Alberni, in August, 1967, I had fish & chips at MARTIN'S. How many of you can remember the VALLEY TRAILER PARK, on Gertrude Street four blocks north of the Alberni Post Office? Did you know that "car top boats" were produced in Alberni? They were, at COLPMAN BOATWORKS on River Road. Ten feet, 2 inches long, constructed of cedar strip and covered with fibreglass, these boats weighed 78 pounds and were capable of speeds up to thirty miles per hour.

More on a Valley Legend... THE LANTERN INN...

Remember I wrote about Don Gunn a few weeks ago? Well now I have uncovered a picture of the original neon sign, when the Lantern Inn started on lower Third Avenue. The picture is from an ad in the September, 1956 issue of "Island Events" magazine. Don and his three partners, John Lee, Len Gunn and John Mah had opened the popular eatery a couple of months earlier. (July 1, 1956)

The original Lantern Inn was destroyed, along with a store, apartment block, garage building and several small houses, in a spectacular fire on Saturday, August 8, 1959. As many of you may recall, I mentioned before that the partners then relocated to Beaver Creek Road, (where Arbutus RV is now) re-opening in November of 1959. It's interesting to note that in 1956, it was advertised that the Lantern Inn was the only restaurant specializing in Chinese Food in this area. They also delivered or "had food ready for collection."

More on that $100,000 blaze in the coming weeks.

MORE ON STIRZAKER'S
New, most modern restaurant on the Island opened April 10, 1947

"Absolutely, definitely, without question," is how Colin Stirzaker answered last Sunday, when I asked him if the picture above was taken shortly after his parents famous restaurant opened in 1947.

The beautiful interior of Stirzaker's on Third Avenue was described in the local press of the day as being "the last word in comfort and convenience". There is seating for 150 in the dining room and the "horse shoe counter" will accommodate 24 patrons, was what the article in the West Coast Advocate proclaimed.

Now, when you look at this picture (obviously taken at night) can you tell me who the employees inside are?

"You can see two fellows on the right," Colin pointed out. "I believe they are Art Bates (Jim's brother) and Joe Hills."

What do you think? Let's discuss it by email at: ikepatterson@telus.net or at 250-723-3709.

About the photo of Stirzaker's that I ran on September 4, the one from the late Thor M. Peterson's collection, Colin confirms that it was taken in 1950, as we originally thought.

"I am sure that the 1950 Chevy, the car in the middle of the picture, was my father's," Colin said. "It was a maroon coloured car and every time I washed it, I had pink hands."

Colin has promised to get me other pictures of this popular eatery that reigned supreme for almost a decade. Watch for more installments on this story in the weeks to come.

***May 7, 1913...A VALLEY DATE TO REMEMBER!!

The birth of the WEST COAST GENERAL HOSPITAL...

A community-drive for a local 20-bed hospital, on Redford Street, actually started in 1908 with a small group of dedicated volunteers from both Alberni and Port Alberni. The dream was realized with the official opening on May 7, 1913. The photo below shows the opening ceremonies by local dignitaries and then-Health Minister Dr. Esson Young, who was quoted by the newspaper of the day as saying "this was a major event in the development of both communities."

Photo courtesy of the Alberni Valley Museum   PN02568

This is what the original West Coast General Hospital looked like in April of 1913, just prior to admitting it's first patients. The insert between the two is where the opening ceremonies were held on May 7th, 1913. See photo opposite.

Photo courtesy of the Alberni Valley Museum

Photo courtesy of the archives.

This is how the West Coast General Hospital looked in 1937 after a new east wing was added in 1926 and the west wing, which was constructed in 1935. You can see on the left of the photo unique fire escape that consisted of a long covered slide on which patients & mattresses could be placed on and slid to safety.

The newly-formed Alberni Board of Trade had put a committee together in 1907 to begin the campaign for a hospital. The board persuaded the then-Alberni Land Company to donate property on Redford Street, which was little more than a trail at the time. Solicitation of funds started, then in June, 1912, the "West Coast General Hospital Society" was formed, which allowed the Board of Trade to gradually withdraw from the project. Two men named Warnoch and Cochrane had the winning tender of $7,605 for construction of the project, and the architect was the Victoria firm of George Mesher, the same company that designed and supervised construction of the Somass Hotel.

Then in February of 1913, fund raising was given a big boost with formation of Ladies Auxiliaries in both towns. WCGH actually started admitting patients on April 13, 1913, but the official opening ceremonies were delayed until May 7.

Later..27 beds were added in 1926 when an east wing was added, then a 20-bed west wing came about in 1935.

Then in 1951 overcrowding and a run-down state of the hospital caused the "unreal, legendary community spirit to resurface as residents came together, again, to raise the local share for a new building, to be built near the original on additional lots bought in 1925 from the Alberni Land Company. Volunteers came up with the $100,000 needed(remember the beard growing and klondike community promotions in the fall of 1948 that I wrote about a number of weeks ago?) and in 1952, the 111-bed, five floor facility was opened by pioneer doctor C.T. Hilton(whose home on Third Avenue became the location for the retail giant Woodward's 4 years earlier)

I'll have more on WCGH IN future columns, including the 1952 and 1972 milestones.

Photo courtesy of the Alberni Valley Museum   PN2216
The building site for the new West Coast General Hospital. Photo taken May 10th, 1951.

It's also nice to know that the extended care facility that was added in 1972 and named after W.H. Prescott(he was the first provincial government appointee to the hospital board of directors and was the only surviving member of the group of pioneers whose dedication and hard work brought the first hospital to life) is still being utilized today as "ABBEYFIELD," the unique home to 19 seniors.

Remembering a very generous donation

The Save the Children Fund of B.C. received one of its largest private donations when a cheque for $112,152 was presented 22 years ago. The money came from the estate of the late Matthew Haller of Port Alberni. Estate executor Dennis Thain, middle, presented the cheque to Fund director Jo Briggs of Duncan on Thursday, July 14 in the offices of the attorney handling the estate, William Beckingham, left, on Thursday, July 14, 1988. For those unfamiliar with the charity, the B.C. branch worked with Save the Children of the United Kingdom to offer medical, social and physical care for children around the world.

Dairy Queen dished up 4,848 sundaes on July 17, 1988

Port Alberni's Dairy Queen originally opened on July 17, 1958 on the corner of 14th Avenue and Redford Street. James Wallace Sr. and Jim Wallace Jr. owned and operated the take-out store until George Flint joined the partnership in June of 1971. Then in February 1972, the new Dairy Queen opened on 3rd Avenue with a dine-in capacity of 72 seats and hot food added to the famous "cool treats" menu.

On Sunday, July 17, 1988, the DQ celebrated 30 years in business with a repeat of the 1958 Grand Opening Sale – a 5-cent sundae sale. Customers waited patiently to buy their first sundae for 20 cents, and get a second for a nickel.

"In all 4,848 sundaes were served between 11 a.m. and midnight, a time when usually about 200 are served," co-owner George Flint, reported. "The day was quite successful. Even though people had to wait in line, they were congenial and offered their congratulations." July 17 also was the official retirement day for co-owner Jim Wallace and the beginning of a Dairy Queen career for Ken Terryberry (Jim's son-in-law).

Also in July 1988
A one dollar ticket becomes $1,698,420 for local man

Port Alberni's John Kutzschan struck it rich on July 27, 1988 when the Lotto 6/49 ticket he had purchased at 7-Eleven made him an instant millionaire.

"It's going to change every minute of every hour for the rest of my life," the retired mill worker told reporters after winning a $1.6 million jackpot. "I checked my tickets, circled each number and there was six of them, all in the right places."

Kutzschan, a 67-year-old single man with no children at the time, said he was going to give $100,000 sums to a few friends and family members and invest the rest in real estate.

"I buy lottery tickets on 80 per cent of the draws, but I never won anything this big before," he added.

A RARE PICTURE SAVED!

John McNabb's stepdaughter, who now works for MacMillan Bloedel's successor, saved this great local photo.

"They were moving offices in Vancouver," John said. "Jacqueline thought we'd like it for our home, so she stopped it from being thrown out."

Although we don't know just when this picture was taken, there are some clues offered that narrow down the years.

"It was before I came to town," John offered. "For one thing there's no Barclay Hotel, and that was being built when I arrived."

Other clues as to the date when the photographer captured this moment are: It had to have been after 1946, because the CJAV studios and transmitter tower are visible at Third & Redford. As John mentioned, there is no sign of the Barclay, next to CJAV, so it was before 1957 when the Barclay officially opened.

Also you can narrow it down a little more. The old "two spot" was given to the City in May 1954, by H.R. MacMillan himself, and was put on display on the northeast corner of Third and Redford. You can't make that out in the photo, so obviously it was taken before '54. I'm thinking the late '40's. What do you think? Send your historical "two bits worth " to me at:
ikepatterson@telus.net.

"One day it should probably go to the Museum," John observed. "It's a pretty cool old picture!"

FINALLY – A FRANKLIN RIVER SCHOOL PICTURE!
Thanks to Werner Krupek for sending in this 1959 photo

Now Franklin River as remembered by Werner Krupek:

Werner came to Franklin River Camp (from Germany) with his mom, Edith Krupek and his two younger brothers, Peter and Harry, in April 1958. His dad, Horst Krupek, was already in Canada working at Franklin River and living in the bunkhouses. He came to Canada to work and save money to bring his wife and young boys over to join him. When the family arrived, they all moved into family housing and lived there for two to three years, until they moved to the big city of Port Alberni.

Werner's youngest brother, Horst, was born in 1959 at West Coast General because there was no hospital at Franklin River. Today Werner's parents and three brothers still all live in Port Alberni. Horst Sr. and Edith just celebrated 50 years of living in Canada this past April.

"My mom wondered where the heck she was going when she came to Franklin River from Vancouver after arriving from Berlin,"

"Mrs. Bledsoe was the teacher and the class consisted of grades 1 to 4," Margo Krupek emailed. "After Werner and I talked to you at the Fall Fair we looked through our old photos and found this one from Franklin River which was taken in 1959. Werner can only remember a few of the kids' names and he isn't sure if the spelling is right. He was in grade 2 and was 7 years old."

Back Row – (left to right): Dennis White, Keith Bennet, Brian or Randy Ball, _____, Mark Goddard, _____, _____ and Werner Krupek.
Second Row: (no names submitted)
Front Row: Keith Ball, _____, _____, Stelmacher boy, _____, _____, _____ and _____.

Werner commented. "She only spoke German and felt like she had arrived on Mars, but in time she learned how to speak English."

The boys also only spoke German but picked up English quite easily while playing with the other kids at camp and at school.

Werner has many happy memories of life at Franklin River and we would like to hear from other former residents of that logging camp in the middle of nowhere. Let's chat about the coffee shop, the community centre and of course, the school that had two classrooms with grades 1 to 7.

A fantastic view of Franklin River Camp B from over 50 years ago

Bob Solderlund, now retired, is well known for his many years of fine work with a camera at the Ha-Shilth-Sa newspaper, dropped by with this unreal aerial shot of Franklin River Camp B at Coleman Creek. He explained that he was in Grade 1 when the family lived there for a short time in the early fifties.

"I was given this picture by my brother Ken years ago," Bob revealed. "I don't know the date it was taken or who the photographer was, but you can see cars parked in the upper right hand side."

This is an important observation because the road to Port Alberni (26 miles away) was completed in December 1954, early '55. This means the picture was taken later in '55 or early in 1956.

"You'll notice the two large car ports beside the road to Port in the bottom of the picture," former Franklin River resident Don Watt pointed out. "They were built prior to 1957, along with the new bunkhouses in the top left of the photo."

In January 2009, I ran quite a few articles and pictures from Don Watt on all three locations of Camp B (Corrigan Creek, Parsons Creek and finally, Coleman Creek, which opened in 1946). Last week, just after I showed Don this picture, he was given a copy of the "Harmac News" from Nanaimo's Bob Hoar, who also lived at Camp B while growing up. That M & B-published Harmac News, dated November 1956, contained a feature story on Franklin River Division, and THIS PICTURE was part of that story.

Well, that defines the timeline of when this picture was taken to between say the spring of 1955 to before the fall of 1956. What do you think? Please take a good look and send your memories to: ikepatterson@telus.net and watch for more memories from Camp B as Don Watt and other former Franklin River residents point out highlights from this rare picture that so clearly shows "the logging camp that had everything."

Local Landmark Lost!

Four months and two days after its 51st birthday, the Alberni Athletic Hall has ceased to exist. The legendary building was completely destroyed in a stunning fire early Wednesday morning.

After news of the fire got out - Port Alberni Fire Department got paged out and responded at 4:28am and arrived at the Hall at 4:32am – people flocked to the scene to watch Firefighters battle the blaze and witness the tragic loss of a Valley icon. The steady stream of fans of the famous facility continued throughout the day and on Wednesday night there was still a constant cavalcade of curious on-lookers driving past the charred ruins on Beaver Creek Road.

When you realize the significant role that the Athletic Hall, which opened on January 11, 1958 – and it's predecessor, the original building constructed in 1931 – played in the lives of thousands of Valley residents over more than seven decades, they deserve special historical recognition, along with the Alberni Athletic Association.

Two years ago, with background from Bill Andrews, a former member of the Alberni Athletic Senior A Men's team who played on January 11, 1958 against the Vancouver Eilers, I wrote an article describing the construction and opening night of the Alberni Athletic Hall fifty-one years ago. Here again is that story:

This submitted photo shows the full fury of the blaze that consumed the Athletic Hall.

Neil Abrahamson, who spent hours at the fire, snapped this shot of the Firefighters still on the scene after daybreak.

The building of the new **ATHLETIC HALL** (the one we have today) was a "major community project" sponsored by the Alberni Athletic Association. A capacity crowd was on hand to witness the opening of the $70,000 hall, which was built with funds raised here in the valley.

It was Saturday, January 11, 1958, but the miraculous story actually began right after the **ATHLETICS** won the Canadian Basketball Championships in 1955, in the original hall, which had been a second home for literally thousands of young athletes of the district. That first Athletic Hall (which was just south of the new building) was built in 1931 and was torn down shortly after the official opening of the magnificent new facility which included the 94 by 50 foot "Eastern Maple playing floor," modern dressing rooms and permanent seating for 800 people.

How it happened...

Ernie Shorter, then General Manager of Western District Operations for MacMillan and Bloedel, suggested that funds, which the Athletic Association was going to use for repairing the old building, become the beginning of a fund for a new building.

MacMillan and Bloedel then promptly made a donation of $10,000 to that fund and gave a generous discount on all lumber to be used on the project. Woodward's Stores put in $1,000, a similar amount in small donations from various businesses, $30,000 raised through bond sales and about $20,000 of Athletic Association funds made it possible to commence building.

Art Bowerman was put in charge of the building committee, with many local firms contributing throughout the project, even the City helped in grading operations and 50 men turned out for the big cement-pouring bee for the foundation. Hundreds of hours of volunteer work, including regular work bees, made the new hall possible.

On opening night...

Fred Bishop, the manager of the Athletics, introduced the speakers and special guests, the first of whom was a former resident and avid basketball fan, the Reverend Harry Greenhalgh, who came from Nanaimo to lead the prayers and dedicate the new hall. According to reports from the Nanaimo Free Press, James Forrest gave a welcoming address on behalf of the Athletic Association. He told the crowd that there was still a lot of work to be done on the hall, which he hoped would be completed in the near future.

Speeches were given by Mayors Loran Jordon and Jack Luckhurst of Port Alberni and Alberni respectively. John Polley, president of the Canadian Amateur Basketball Association, said "although it's pleasing to have a new hall, we leave behind, in the old one, a lot of happy memories that lead up to the Canadian championship." Then he made a comment that history would make come true in 1965, "Wouldn't it be a wonderful thing, if in this new hall, we could once again win the championship."

Basil Sands, president of the BCABA, said "Nowhere in B.C. does any basketball team have such good supporters as the Alberni Athletics."

Ernie Shorter, who was promoted to Vice-President of MacMillan and Bloedel, said he was only too pleased that his firm had helped the cause financially.

Following the opening remarks, the majorettes and the high school band led a parade of 175 teams onto the floor. They ranged from pre-midgets to the original players of the first Athletic team.

There was a series of short games involving minor divisions and "happy memories were brought back for old-time spectators when George "Porky" Andrews took the toss up for the Vancouver Eilers versus the "A" game. That game, played on the one of the best basketball floors in Western Canada, was won by the "A's" 58-41.

The evening closed with a game between the Senior "B" team and Vancouver Wallace, which ended with a 49-45 victory for Wallace.

Port Alberni Toy Run – the early years

Dave Dagg (left) and Perry Shepard flank Lt. Denny Fahrenholtz of the Salvation Army with the 40 odd toys collected in the first annual Toy Run by local motorcycle enthusiasts and supporters.

It all started back in the fall of 1985 when 25 riders and about a dozen passengers escorted nearly 40 individual toys from the Alberni Mall to the Scout Hall on Montrose Street.

The AV Junior Chamber of Commerce sponsored that first "Toy Run", which, under escort from the RCMP, took the Redford Extension and followed Redford down to Third Avenue in procession, turning through the downtown area to the final destination, where Lt. Denny Fahrenholtz of the Salvation Army collected the toys as the first installment on the annual Sally Ann drive.

"It was a really good feeling, because it was everybody doing something for the good," said Dave Dagg, who co-chaired the event with Perry Shepard. "We'll be doing it again next year."

On October 25, 1986, sixty-five local motorcyclists attached toys to their bikes and toured from Cathedral Grove to the Fall Fairground Kin Hut. That year 400 toys were donated to the Salvation Army's Christmas Hamper Fund.

The turnout was better than ever for the Alberni Valley Jaycee's third annual toy drive on Oct. 24, 1987. About 120 to 140 motorcyclists took part, including bikers from all over Vancouver Island and the Lower Mainland. Organizers estimated the amount of toys and cash was tripled from the previous year. Some 475 toys were loaded into the Salvation Army van along with a cheque for $1,225 following the 1988 Toy Run. The sun shone brightly as more than 140 motorcyclists made the ride from Cathedral Grove. Besides attracting riders from all parts of the province, the local committee managed to more than double every aspect of the run, especially the number of warm-hearted merchants who contributed to the event.

Thanks to the hard work of those dedicated local volunteers in the beginning, and each year since, the Port Alberni Toy Run has continued and grown. Almost 1,200 bikes hit the highway in 2009 and more are expected to participate this Saturday. Yes, the distinct roar of all makes of motorcycles (some say it's the original thunder in the Valley) will be heard coming down Johnston about noon on Saturday (they leave Little Qualicum Falls at 11:00 a.m.). The route goes like this; they turn left onto Gertrude, down Kingsway, circling the fountain at the Harbour Quay, up Argyle to Tenth, then down to the Fall Fairgrounds.

It is a sight to see – and hear! As you watch, remember it's for the kids, just like it was back in 1985.

You're bound to recognize these members of the 1987 Toy Run Committee.

Members of the Toy Run Committee with some of the 400 toys donated in the 1986 event. Dave Dagg, project president (top left) is pictured here with organizers of the charity event (not in order) Perry Shepard, Bert Dufour, Brian Loudan, Johnny Versteeg, Randal Dafoe, Harry Cross and Fred Race.

Please note** The winning ticket in this year's Ty Watson House ATV raffle will be drawn at 4:30 p.m. this Saturday, Sept. 18, during the Toy Run rodeo at Glenwood Center. For details on the draw, the raffle or Ty Watson House, please contact the AV Hospice Office at 250-723-4478 or visit the Society's website: www.albernihospice.ca

Tidal Waves Spare Life in Albernis

That was the headline in the Daily Colonist on Sunday, March 29, 1964

45 years later, those who experienced it, still remember the damaging 'Tsunami' that occurred following a Good Friday earthquake near Anchorage, Alaska. The Colonist reported, among many other things, how "rampaging tidal waves swept up the Alberni Inlet early Saturday Morning (March 28) creating havoc on the waterfront and low-lying areas of Alberni and Port Alberni. The first wave struck shortly after midnight and at 1:35 a.m. at high tide, a 16-foot wave, increasing in force as it rushed 40 miles down the narrow channel, sent water crashing over the assembly wharf, swelling over the banks of the Somass River to homes in the low-lying River Road area of Alberni and surging through several blocks of downtown Port Alberni. *

The third wave at 3:50 a.m. was much reduced in strength, and the fourth, at 4:15 a.m., was neutralized by low tide."   * (actually lower Third Avenue).

Much has been written over the years about the Tidal Wave, the millions of dollars in damage it caused and the very remarkable community recovery effort (assisted by donations from virtually everywhere), but I think it definitely deserves our attention this weekend. What do you think? Were you here at the time? Did you find out later on that Saturday morning that something had happened? Did you get called by a distant relative wondering if you were okay?

This picture was taken at first light on Saturday, March 28, 1964 and it is one of several highly recognizable shots that appeared in newspapers all over the world. The wrecked Rambler at the Riverside Auto Court (now the location of Clutesi Haven Marina) belonged to British visitors Wilf and Shirley Smith, who had come to Canada eight months before and were with relatives on their first trip to Vancouver Island.

ON A PERSONAL NOTE:::

I first heard of the Alberni Valley forty-one years ago, along with millions of others around the world. A Tidal Wave (as it was called then) or Tsunami, resulting from the Alaskan earthquake which measured 8.4 on the Richter scale, had struck the twin cities of Alberni and Port Alberni. The fact that such an event had happened so close to home (I grew up in Squamish) was stunning, but as more information became available two other facts impressed me to no end. One, there was no loss of life, and two, the manner in which everyone had pulled together to get through the night and the immediate aftermath. Who could have guessed it at the time, but three years later I was here working at "the voice of the Alberni Valley." Although I wasn't here at the time, I did a lot of research and along with a couple of "on air" colleagues, produced a "radio docu-drama" which aired in the '80's. The realism of the show, helped out by a power outage near the beginning, caused quite a stir in the community, and the outside media made mention of it, but more on that in future weeks. What follows has been taken directly from the "ALBERNI VALLEY AND WEST COAST DISASTER FUND" Flyer, a government sponsored relief drive, for which income tax-deductible contributions could be made at any bank or credit union in BC. I recall the late Fred Bishop telling me that money and offers of assistance had been coming in from all over Canada even before this fund raising drive started.

TIDAL WAVE!

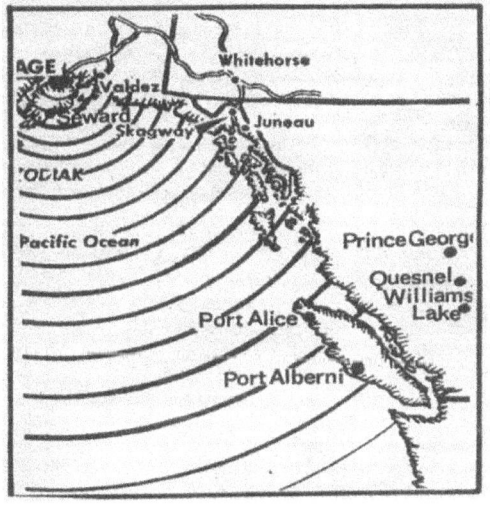

The foggy dawn of Saturday, March 28, 1964, broke on a stunned and unbelieving populace in the Alberni Valley. Residents were stunned by the small glimpse they'd already had of the fantastic damage done to their communities . . . unbelieving at the reports that no one had been drowned or even seriously injured in the tidal wave which swept the low-lying areas in the midnight hours following the great Alaska earthquake.

Other communities up and down the west coast of North America felt in varying degrees the effects of the tidal waves which followed the northern upheaval. But the length and shape of the same Alberni Inlet which cleaves 35 miles through the heart of Vancouver Island on British Columbia's coast, and which is the very reason for the existence of the twin cities of Alberni and Port Alberni, also ordained that they should suffer greatly from the tidal wave.

Along most sections of the coast the first eight foot wave rolled past almost unnoticed.

But in the narrowing confines of Alberni Inlet, the water was forced to pile up, and the first wave equalled the worst flooding conditions ever recorded here. The second was several feet higher, and rolled in with more force.

Where the first wave served to alert the communities just enough to prevent loss of life, the second marched inland to carry off homes, automobiles and the pathetic personal remainders strewn about by any disaster. The waterfront industries (plywood, lumber, pulp and paper) on which the towns depend for their livelihood were knocked out; businesses in the lower areas were swamped.

The period of grace between the first wave and the disastrous second was not long enough to get everyone moving toward safety . . . many were caught in their homes. The fast-rising waters knocked out all power and street lighting, so that many waded chest-deep, in the sudden dark, through their yards to safety.

For visitors staying in some of the auto courts near the river, there was the added complication of finding their way over strange ground . . . yet all made it to higher areas.

Even more miraculous were some of the hair-breadth escapes of children. One man dashed out to save his brand-new convertible only to find a pair of youngsters floating by on a log; he too was chest deep before the trio made it to dry ground. A civil defense worker rowing around in the dark checking houses flashed his light into one, and rescued a baby floating on a mattress.

The tales of close escapes are endless, and days later people who witnessed the tidal flood still found it hard to believe there'd been no casualties.

But as time went by after the waters had receded the tally of damage went up and up. Some 58 properties . . . individual homes, stores and multiple auto courts . . . were assessed as 100% losses. Hotels, motels, stores, car lots, warehouses and service stations all suffered staggering losses in stock and furnishings.

As the figures came in from damage survey teams, the total mounted to some $5,000,000 in losses to homes and businesses alone. This sum does not include the huge damage totals of the waterfront industries, lost production or lost payrolls, nor does it include the hundreds of thousands of dollars in claims for salt-soaked cars and trucks.

This picture shows residents walking down River Road toward Alberni. Notice the house and the boat on the road.

This photo shows the mess in front of the old Barclay Hotel near Third & Redford. CJAV was located in the hotel at the time, instead of the original studios on the extreme right of the picture.

Coming soon to these pages..
- From 1953..Paul Hertel's Cougars
- From 1957..The old Calgary School Fire
- From 1964..The first Rolf Harris Concert in Port Alberni
- From 1965..The 2nd Canadian Basketball Championship for the Alberni Athletics

Do you have any story ideas you'd like to see in This Was Then, contact Ike at The Pennyworth - 723-3709 or email pennywrth@shaw.ca

The Two Spot plaque is back
Missing historical memento saved from on-line auction block

Museum director Jean McIntosh looks over the commemorative brass plaque that was on the Two Spot locomotive when H.R. MacMillan presented it to the City of Port Alberni 56 years ago.
A railroad enthusiast who bought it at a flea market in Vancouver around 1980 returned the 35x40 cm artifact, which weighs approximately 10 kilograms. [Ike Patterson, Pennyworth]

H.R. MacMillan addressed the crowd gathered at the corner of Third and Redford at 11 a.m. on May 24, 1954 during the dedication ceremony for the Two Spot. The red arrow points to the spot where the recovered plaque was originally on the "Deuce", as the Two Spot was sometimes called. Port Alberni Mayor Loran Jordan, third from the right on the platform, accepted the 42-ton gift from the chairman of the Board of MacMillan Bloedel.
This picture, which was given to me long before I created This Was Then, aroused my interest during my search for history on CJAV Radio. My former boss, the late Ken Hutcheson, can be seen in the bottom right hand corner. Behind Ken, you can see part of Tom Rannie, another popular radio announcer here at the time. [Photo from Ike Patterson's collection]

It's an amazing story

You could say, "It's the Shay still talked about today." The Two Spot is really the little engine that could, and did. It has been documented that the locomotive (manufactured in 1912) entered the Alberni Valley as a new machine in 1914 and served faithfully until 1953 when she was replaced by truck hauling. As written on the brass dedication plaque recovered after more than 30 years, Two Spot hauled many millions of feet of logs from the forests to Port Alberni mills. After it was saved from the scrap heap, and officially presented to the City in 1954, the Two Spot sat on display, on rails manufactured in 1871, at Redford and Stamp Avenue. Its operating days were over, so everyone thought. After all, its boiler tubes had been removed.
No one would have guessed 56 years ago that one day, old Two Spot would return to the rails locally and even steam to world fame at Expo 86 in Vancouver. Well, thanks to a handful of "railroaders" and tremendous community support, the Two Spot was restored and made a triumphant return to work under her own power on August 11, 1984. Costly repairs forced the retirement of the Two Spot in 1994, but the group of enthusiasts who lovingly restored her dream of the day the funds can be raised to put her back on the tracks again. When that day comes, the dedication plaque will take its rightful place on the cab once more.

Were you at Stepping Stones Day Care 25 years ago?

Children of the Stepping Stones Day Care helped out in the official ceremony for Child Safety Week in Port Alberni back in April 1986. The kids took time on Friday, April 4 for a photo op with McGruff the Crime Dog, Mayor Gillian Trumper and RCMP Constable Barb Alexander. Parents and youngsters may recall the highlight of Child Safety Week twenty-five years ago was free fingerprinting and photographing of children in the Alberni Mall on the Friday evening and all day Saturday. If you see yourself in this picture, please let me know at: ikepatterson@telus.net

Its Salmon Festival weekend – for the 39th time
Recalling the first winners

Left: This picture of Fred McLeod, the Salmon Festival's first big winner, was actually taken in August of 1973, as he was warming up for the second derby. Fred, who landed a 45 pound, 11 ounce tyee to claim the $5,000 first prize in the 1972 Festival, unfortunately failed to make it two-in-a-row.

Right: Gil Dore was wearing the $5,000 smile in 1973, thanks to the 52 pounds, two ounces winner that he caught off Nahmint Bay. Gil's big one remained the record holder until 1982 when Art Berlinski won the Salmon Festival with a beauty weighing 60 pounds, eight ounces. Art still has the distinction of catching the largest fish ever to win the annual derby.

Lake Cowichan's Wayne Harvey with his 1974 first-prize fish, a 49 pound, four ounce salmon he caught at Coleman Creek and the unique tyee-shaped $5,000 cheque.

And, here is an early derby shot of Cory Jones, last year's Salmon Festival winner.

Cory was 9 years old when he caught this salmon weighing 40 pounds, 4 ounces off Home Island in 1981. The fish that year was almost as big as Cory, and not much smaller than the 43 pound, 4 ounce catch he landed last year to win the '09 Salmon Festival.
Cory will be out on the water again this year, so we might see a two-in-a-row winner before the 40th derby next year.

Remembering Fred McLeod - Salmon Festival's first big winner

Port Alberni's Fred McLeod, left, happily receives his $5,000 salmon-shaped cheque from Times publisher Fred Duncan after winning the 1972 Port Alberni Salmon Festival. That very first festival was co-sponsored by the AV Times and McDonald's Export 'A' and the closing ceremonies were held at 5p.m. on the grounds of the Greenwood Motor Hotel, derby headquarters.

Everyone, who was here on Labour Day weekend 38 years ago, will undoubtedly recall how Fred McLeod reeled in his 45 pound, 11 ounce catch in the early hours of the first day, then had to sweat it out until 3 p.m. on Monday when fishing closed.

And, you may remember the second prize in the first Salmon Festival ever held, was won by 16-year old ADSS student, Kim Cote, who won a 12 foot boat, trailer and 25 horsepower motor with his 40 pound, six ounce salmon.

It was the summer of 1990

Miss Port Alberni Tanya Versteeg and Princess Jonquil Parisian wave from the award-winning Chamber of Commerce "Community with a Heart" float during the Folkfest parade on Sunday, July 1, 1990. The spectacular float won the Best Non-Commercial Entry and captured the Grand Overall award in the parade, which included 41 entries and was seen by hundreds of people.

Also during the summer of 1990

- **United Buy and Sell Furniture Warehouse** opened for business on July 19, and Darryl Lewis was the manager.
  "There has been a very good response," he told reporters a week after the opening. "About half the customers who come in here say that it was about time a store like this came into Port Alberni."
- **Steve and Sharon Mooney** officially opened a Remax (Realty Maximum) outlet on Third Avenue on Friday, July 20. Over 80 guests celebrated the arrival of the new firm with a wine and cheese party.
- **Port Alberni first met the Frances Barkley** on Saturday, August 11, 1990 when it arrived after a 9,000-mile journey from Stavanger, Norway. The 128-foot ship, purchased to relieve some the Lady Rose's workload, was sailed here by Brooke George and his crew who had flown to Norway in April.

A Big Fish Story From 1949.....
(As it appeared in the Nanaimo Free Press)
73 1/2-POUND SALMON TAKEN ON HAND LINE
Port Alberni, Sept. 3--Sidney Thomas Henley of Sarita River has caught the largest Tyee salmon ever taken on hook and line in Alberni inlet waters. The huge fish weights 73 and a half pounds, was 53 and 3/4 inches long and 33 1/2 inches in girth. Confirmation of the size of the fish has been made by Pitt Clayton, chairman of the Alberni District Chamber of Commerce. The fish was weighed on engineering scales at Sarita River and was on exhibition for two days. The fish was caught Sunday on a hand line near Kildonan Harbour.

STOP THE PRESSES! THE REAL STORY OF HOW THE TWIN CITIES TIMES STARTED.

Last September, after the AV Times published an article about the paper's history, Jim Adams came to see me proclaiming it wasn't correct.
"I should know," Jim insisted. "I was there. As a matter of fact I had the first copies of the first two issues for the longest time, before I gave them to the archives."
It turns out that Jim was the "printer's devil" for Oliver L'ami when the Twin Cities Times first hit the streets in December, 1946.
Jim can remember very well working for Nelson Ball when the weekly paper was first printed in the basement of Ball's house on 5th Avenue.
Well, I went to see Ann Holt at the local archives, and here is a copy of the first page of the first issue of the Twin Cities Times, dated December 10, 1946.

I also uncovered an article written by Oliver L'Ami's son Terry, who related:

"After several editions improved publishing arrangements had to be found," he wrote. "Father finally arranged with the Nanaimo Free Press to handle his copy and to print a weekly press run every Sunday for him."

According to Terry both his mother and father took up full duties to gather stories, report the news and sell advertising. Each day the material was assembled and shipped to Nanaimo by bus so the Free Press staff could compose it in advance. Then early each Sunday morning the L'Amis would be in Nanaimo supervising the printing of their weekly edition, returning in the evening with a 1946 Ford sedan full of Twin Cities Times. The family would then prepare the copies for Monday's mailing.

"This became a ritual for around two years," Terry wrote. "Then it became obvious that a printing press installed in Port Alberni was not going to happen.

Eventually the business side of the venture failed with just too many costs and not enough paid-for advertisements. So my father's little dream died a silent death and he sold out to the local bank manager, Fred Duncan, and became the editor of the Nanaimo Free Press.

The name Oliver L'Ami is also listed in local history records as being one of the first employees of CJAV when it went on the air in April of 1946.

More about Oliver L'Ami, Fred Duncan and the Twin Cities Times in future columns. If you have anything to add, please email to: ikepatterson@telus.net or call 723-3709.

Anyone who has lived in Port Alberni for any length of time remembers 1964 as the year of the "Tidal Wave" or Tsunami.

But can you recall local businesses from 1964, that no longer exist?
HAYS ROOFING & CHIMNEY SERVICE, ARROW KIRK COAL that was on Roger Street, or PORT ALBERNI HOME BUILDERS located on 4th Avenue North. WEST COAST CONCRETE WORKS was operating on Beaver Creek Road back in '64, and Albina Major owned the Alberni Delicatessen on Margaret Street, where Big Pig Subs is today.

When it came to Department Stores, we had WOODWARD'S, WOOLWORTH'S, ZELLERS, LAVERS, EATON'S, and WEBBER ROBINSON. There was no shortage of Drug Stores either, including two CUNNINGHAMS locations, WATSON'S PHARMACY, MACDONALD REXALL DRUGS, MCKINNELL DRUGS LTD., AND WOODWARD'S STORES DRUGS. Somass Drugs is the only one still operating that was in business in 1964.

Can you still remember THE ALBERNI FLORIST on Margaret? What about NELSON'S LAUNDERERS & DRY CLEANERS on 4th Avenue South? HELEN'S HOBBY & ROCK SHOP is a name you don't hear anymore. COMPTON'S JEWELLERS, PORT SHIPPING, KAY'S LADIES APPAREL, ROSE LANE LADIES WEAR, and DEVOY'S GROCERY are never talked about anymore. A lot of local businesses have literally disappeared since 1964, but hey, that was 43 years ago.

***November 18, 1947..A Valley Date to Remember!!
Worst Fire for Casualties in Port History Most Guests Accounted for But Crews Probing Hotel Ruins For Further Possible Victims

That was the headline and sub-headlines in the Thursday, November 20, 1947 edition of the West Coast Advocate. The story went on to say that the fire which completely destroyed the King Edward Hotel at Port Alberni early Tuesday morning was one of the worst in the city's history as far as loss of life and injuries are concerned. Property loss is estimated at $85,000. One man is dead, nine people were taken to hospital, and at presstime fear was still held that other bodies may still be in the ruins. The police were told the alarm was put in by a waitress at the Starlight Cafe, who was notified of the fire by a customer. Witnesses reported "unearthly screeching" and a woman's cries for help before the fire department arrived. Most injuries, other than burns, were received as panic-stricken occupants jumped from upper windows. Angry flames, feeding upon the tinder-dry frame structure, swept through the 20-room building in a matter of minutes.

This picture, from Old Ike's collection, shows the volunteer firemen keeping the blaze under control. Newspaper reports say "the efficient efforts of the Port Alberni Fire Department kept the fire from spreading to neighboring buildings, although the heat was so intense that paint on buildings across the street was blistered. The flames died down around 4am, but the blackened ruins kept smouldering well into mid-morning."

This photo, also from Old Ike's collection, shows what a stylish building the King Edward Hotel was before the fire. "I would like to thank the Alberni District Historical Society for the assistance with archival material."

It was Tuesday, March 11, 1952 when fire took the Port Theatre

"Blaze Destroys Pioneer Buildings" was the headline in the West Coast Advocate two days after the devastating fire that struck First Avenue 58 years ago. Thanks to Ray Cyr's sister-in-law, Jeannine "Bubbles" Cyr (who was married to Horace), we can look back to when some legendary businesses were lost forever.

The Port Theatre, which had closed down in January 1952 when the new Paramount opened, disappeared along with the adjacent building that housed Spooner's Café and upstairs the Eagles Hall. Next to that, the Port Alberni Billiard Hall and a Rooming House were also destroyed.

The loss of the famous Port Theatre, which was originally built in 1909, made this "conflagration"(as fires were often called then) one of the most memorable blazes for generations of Valley folks.

These pictures are perfect examples of the memories hidden away, sometimes in forgotten photo albums. Once again, I urge you to look over old pictures, and then contact me so everyone can share the history of where we live. As always I can be reached at: ikepatterson@telus.net or you can leave a message for me at 250-723-8171.

This view of the fire was taken from the west side of First Avenue, near Argyle. You can see the Kingsway Hotel down at the end of the block.

Remember when we had a Pizza Patio?

Jack Gauthier was the manager when Pizza Patio opened downtown on Thursday, September 25, 1975. Jack welcomed customers as the doors opened at 11 a.m. that day. Many folks will recall that Pizza Patio was located at 3127 3rd Avenue, next to the old Courthouse Racquet Club building (a short distance from the corner of 3rd & Argyle).

In this shot, you are looking south on First, toward Argyle Street. The Good Eats Café and Alberni Hardware are visible on the left hand side of the picture.

"SOME HOUSES YOU JUST SKIP, BUT NEVER YOURS"
Remembering 25 scary years at Howie Dorn's Haunted House

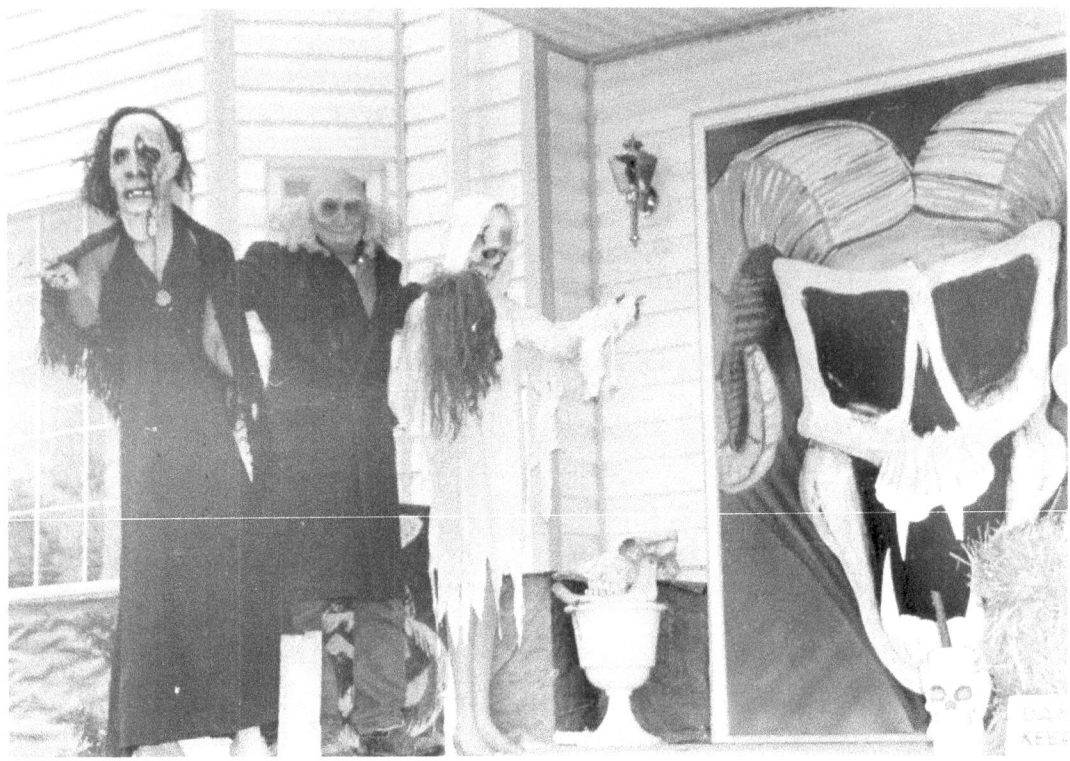

Generations of young trick or treaters grew up believing there was only one truly haunted house in Port Alberni – Howie Dorn's – on First Avenue. Heck, it became a tradition, an honour even to say you got scared at Howie's house on Halloween night.

Not only did Howie and what became known as "his company" of volunteers put on a bigger and better "scare-fest" each year for 25 years they handed out literally thousands of goodie bags.

"The first year, man that was cheese," Howie told me. "We had cardboard tomb stones and a couple of masks. But boy I had fun scaring my nephews from down the street, who were 6,9, and 10 years old." The following year it was better, as Howie recalled, because the dozen or so neighborhood kids the first year told their friends and so on.

"The second year we had huge goodie bags and the annual fright night started snowballing from there." Howie proudly pointed out. "I would get ideas in the middle of summer for Halloween and start building or making stuff – secretly because kids are smart, they remember everything – every year you had to come up with something different. That's tough to do for 25 years."

Tough as it was, Howie played the role of supreme scare master until last year, when he hung up the costumes and props for good so to speak.

25 years worth of bodies, props and costumes were donated to North Island College. The train station became the new venue for scary times as well as allowing the proceeds to be put into North Island college scholarship funds for local students.

WATCH FOR FALLING ROCK....November 14, 1948

I have mentioned ANGEL ROCK before, but I have had numerous requests to re-visit it, so here goes. Thanks to the late Irving Wilson(who's father owned the West Coast Advocate up until 1967) here are my souvenir photos of that famous "picture in time" when the highway around Cameron Lake was changed without man's help and with no loss of life. The weather had apparently weakened the rock face over the years and in the wee hours of the morning, ANGEL ROCK simply dropped. The road was closed for a few days. The first picture shows how the road looked before November 14, 1948, the second photo was taken after daybreak on the 14th. Something to think about on your trip to Nanaimo.

***June 25, 1993....
A Valley Date To Remember!!

ATTENTION CUSTOMERS:
WOODWARD'S
will be
CLOSING
Friday, June 25, 9:00pm

I have mentioned when the Third Avenue Woodward's store first opened several times (March 1, 1948) but recently a man asked me when it had closed. Well, back into my "archives" for the original flyer headline circulated by the management just prior to the final hour, 9pm, Friday, June 25, 1993. The store re-opened as Zellers in mid-September and still is today.

Under Old Business...

When you were shopping on Third Avenue, downtown, in 1973, you would have seen **ROSE LANE LADIES WEAR, ROBBIE'S ROOST, GARY'S SHOES, EATON'S OF CANADA, SIMPSONS-SEARS LTD, THE NOOTKA HOUSE, DICK'S MARKET, YESOWICK'S SPORTING GOODS, FLETCHERS FURNITURE & APPLIANCES**, and of course **WOODWARD'S**.

Missing now in North Port, but alive and well in 1973 were **BRONSON'S HARDWARE, JACK & JILL CHILDREN'S WEAR, THE ALBERNI YARN BARN, ALBERNI VOLKSWAGEN LTD., PORT CONCRETE PRODUCTS(1971)LTD., MR. MIKES, McKAY'S APPAREL**, and **THE SWEET SHOP**. Also gone but not forgotten from 1973..**McKINNON'S DAIRY** on the Nanaimo Highway, **MODERN TUNE-UP CENTRE** on Tenth Avenue, **REBER REALTY** on Argyle, **LARRY'S** Custom Burgers on Gertrude, **THE LANTERN INN** on Beaver Creek Road, **COMMUNITY COLOUR CENTRE & BUILDING SUPPLIES** on Bute Street, **THE VILLAGE SHOPPE** Ladies Fashions in the plaza shopping centre, **VALLEY ROCKGAS** on Fourth Avenue, and **VERN TROMBLEY REPAIR SERVICE** on Fifth Avenue, just to mention a few.

What do you mean when you say nothing ever changes around here??

From Jim Gislason's family photo album
A 63-year old rare picture of legendary Angel Rock

Angel Rock was memorable to anyone who drove around Cameron Lake for decades before November 1948. It was an icon! Thanks to Jim Gislason's parents, we can look back on how impressive Angel Rock really was.

"I'm going through more of my parents old photos," Jim wrote last week. "I found one of my dad Carl, standing by his car at Angel Rock. He said he used to have a '30 Nash, that might be it.

My mom, Mabel, took the picture in November 1948 – my sister was born on Nov. 6, and I thought the rock came down near that time – I'm sure you know the date for sure."

Jim, Angel Rock fell during the early morning hours of November 14, 1948 (as reported in This Was Then many times over the years). It is still regarded as somewhat of a miracle today that no one was killed when "the cave-in" occurred (sometime after midnight on Sunday, November 14).

"I never realized how low that thing was, guess they didn't have semi trucks back then, and I didn't know there were power lines running there either," Jim added.

Folks may recall that in 1977, the Highways Dept. gave Angel Rock a face-lift, shaving the edges off, which allowed bigger trucks an easier and safer trip around Cameron Lake.

Another Alberni Valley Museum "moment"

The Port Alberni Chapter of the Chinese Freemasons Society presented a lion headdress and two ceremonial drums to the AV Museum 21 years ago. The items originally came from Hong Kong and were first used by the Vancouver Chapter of the Chinese Freemasons Society before being brought to Port Alberni in the 1960's. A declining membership here at the time was the reason for the donation according to Don Gunn, who represented the local Chinese Freemasons. Don is seen, along with Jean McIntosh of the Museum in the picture on the right, which appeared in the AV Times on Jan. 12, 1990.

"The items donated back then are still on display in our upstairs gallery," Jean, now the Museum director, confirmed this week.

By the way, the Chinese New Year (Year of the Rabbit) falls on February 3 this year.

***May 12, 1906...A Valley Date to Remember!!
Bob Hutchison Drove the First Auto to the Valley!

Photo courtesy of The Alberni Valley Museum

The arrival of the first automobile in the Alberni Valley is celebrated outside of the Somass Hotel in 1906. A lot of you may remember the Somass began in 1896 as the "Hotel Armour," built for the partnership of Chalmer and Armour. It was 1902, four years before this photo was taken, that Jim Rollins took over the hotel and renamed it THE SOMASS. Rollins would go on to open the KING EDWARD HOTEL in November of 1907.

Thanks to Vic Laughlin's family, I have discovered an article about Bob Hutchison, who brought the first automobiles to Vancouver Island. According to Ron Newton, who wrote the story that appeared in the August 17, 1976 issue of the Arrowsmith Star, Hutchison, an enterprising Victoria man was introducing motor cars to Victoria and the rest of the Island. After he and his brother secured a carload of Oldsmobiles, Hutchison decided to drive the single-cylinder, 8 horsepower model to Port Alberni from Victoria hoping to prove that the autos could be used on stage coach lines. A story in a 1937 issue of the West Coast Advocate related how Hutchison's first part of the maiden journey, from Victoria to Nanaimo, took about eight and a half hour, including stops. Hutchison was a little put off by the experience, so he left the Olds in Nanaimo and returned to Victoria, but three weeks later he was back and completed the run to Port Alberni in four hours and 30 minutes, with a passenger, Mr. Walter Thompson, then the operator of horse-drawn stage coach business. Here's how the Advocate article described that historic ride:::

> The Advocate article says the intrepid duo had little trouble on their trip until just before they reached Cameron Lake.
> There they ran into more horses, and several scenes were caused when the animals bolted on their owners. Rough bridges and culverts also shook the automobilers up--so badly, in fact, that Thompson got out and walked.
> Not one to let his mission falter, Hutchison went on alone until the car balked and finally quit on the steepest part of the old Dog Creek hill. When the engine had cooled down, he started it up again and walked beside the car as it slowly chugged its way over the summit. There he waited for Thompson and the pair rode into Port Alberni in triumph.

In 1903 mass-manufactured autos were first produced and marketed in British Columbia, selling at the low price of $650. Bob Hutchison's first carload of vehicles were tiller steered, curved-dash runabouts and two cylinder touring cars and were hard to sell. No one wanted to pay the full price for any car, so they had to be sold on the installment plan.

Wednesday, June 20, 1973 Hunter's Store, also known as the Sproat Lake Store, burns to the ground. Look for more on this story in weeks to come.

The Lantern Inn Story Continues....

Back to that hot Summer night in 1959. Saturday, August 8, to be exact, when a spectacular fire claimed the original Lantern Inn, on lower Third Avenue. Last week I showed a picture of the neon sign that used to hang above the Inn's door, and this week I have two photos showing the fire itself, which broke out shortly before 5:40 pm. These were taken from the other side of Third, near where Molly Motors used to be, and they truly show the early stages of the furious blaze that claimed the Lantern Inn, Wing's Grocery, an apartment block, garage building and several small houses, causing an estimated $100,000 damage.

These "pictures in time" are from an avid "this was then" fan's photo album, who was there, so to speak, she "waited on tables" at the Lantern Inn in 1957. The shots clearly show how fierce the fire was burning in the back of the building, which would confirm the newspaper reports of the day that said " Unofficially, the fire is thought to have started in the kitchen of the Inn and spread rapidly, fanned by a 20-mile south wind." The reports in the August 10, 1959 issue of the Nanaimo Daily Free Press also mentioned "The blaze is said to have been one of the most destructive in the Valley, more spectacular than that of the Bronson fire in Alberni nearly one year ago." The Bronson fire, that's another story, but for now thank you to "M" for the memories.

CJAV, 1240 AM "The Early Days"

Ever since I arrived at CJAV, in August, 1967, I was researching the past history of what was "one of the hardest radio stations to get a job at." I was told by my instructors at broadcoasting school that I could learn a lot from some of the best "radio people in the industry" if I was lucky enough to get my start here. Well that happened and a spent 28 and ½ years "on the air", probably the senior CJAV staffer, other than the late Bill Gibson, who started in 1956 while in high school and staying until selling the station in 1995. Needless to say, I recorded dozens of inter4views and amassed memorable photos of CJAV AM. Sixty years later, CJAV is known as The Peak at 93.3 FM, but each week this month I'll highlight the years on 1240 AM. The Photo above was handed to me almost thirthy years ago, and it was taken during a birthday part on November 6, 1948, in the original studios at Third & Redford. The announcer cutting the cake, on the left is Chuck Rudd, who went on to CHUB when it started in Nanaimo a year or so later.

When our Library turned 60 years old

It was Thursday, May 30, 1996 when the 60th anniversary party was held for the Port Alberni Branch of the Library at Echo Centre. Were you there? The Scottish Country Dancers performed at the celebrations and children's storyteller Derek Hanebury delighted the younger crowd.

Candy Whytock was the Librarian then, and her assistants were Dorothy Nixdorf, Veronica Hebert, Isabel Caron, Geneva Crowley, and Colleen Chomeakwich.

Mayor Gillian Trumper, left, regional district representative and board member Gary Swann cut the anniversary cake with the help of Penny Grant, Assistant Director of Public Services for the Vancouver Island Regional Library.

CJAV, 1240 AM "The Early Days Continued!!"

When I first set eyes on Port Alberni in August, 1967, it was for a job interview. The studios were on upper Third Avenue, on the second floor above HFC and the barber shop.(odgers and the community police station are there now) Bill Gibson was the announcer, it was just after 1pm, the station had gone off the air, so my interview was conducted driving around with Bill, looking for "Marty", CJAV'S engineer at the time.

A week later Maurice Inwards called me at my home in Squamish, asking if I could be back in a week to start. So, my first night shift(5pm till midnight) was on August 24, 1967. I worked with John Thompson, Ron Coull, Mo of course, Keith Rodgers ** and Ken Hutcheson. Christine Andrews was the front desk receptionist and Irene Maskell was the accountant. There were a few "part-timers" as well. This month, as we continue to recognize 60 years of local radio, I want to feature many of the voices that became Valley household names during the '60's on CJAV 1240 AM.

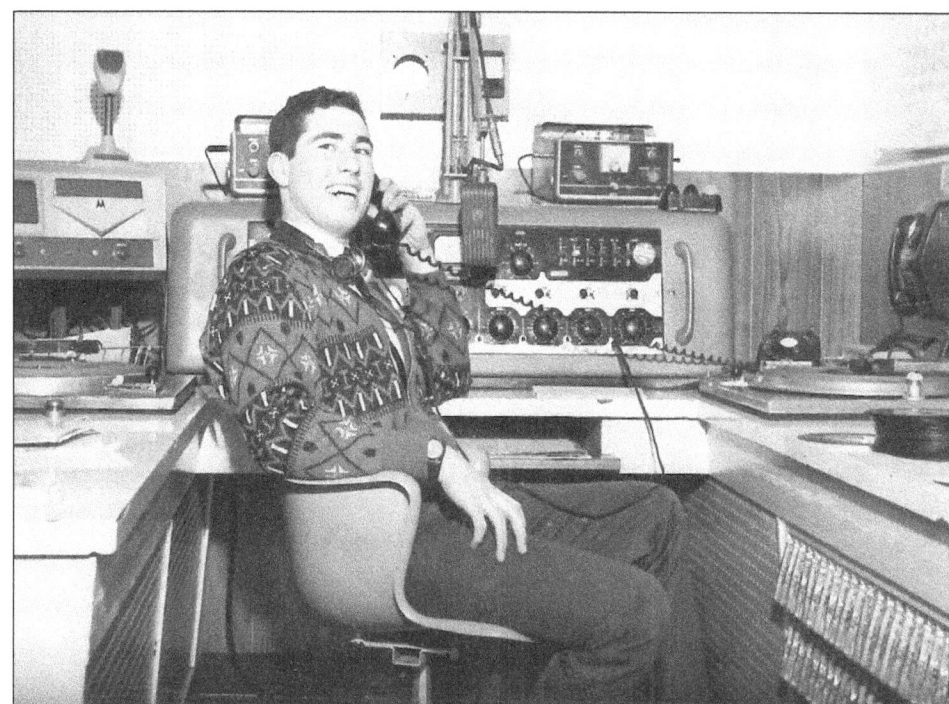

Anton Snikkers was one of the very first people I met after arriving at CJAV in 1967. Anton (who was a popular professional photographer) took this photo the second night I was on the air. Before I came to 1240, Dave Tierney, Bill Coombs, and Pat Nicholson had spent time behind the microphone in the '60's. John Merrett, John Harper and Larry Rose would join us later.

And remember "Old" Ike's lawn mowing contest which ran from 1968 until 1976.

KEN HUTCHESON
Melody Lane 1-3 pm

BILL GIBSON
6 - 9 am

MAURICE INWARDS
Name The Famous

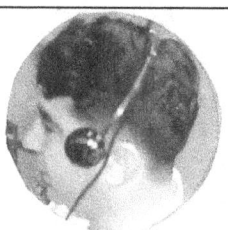
RON COULL
Party Line - Local News

BRIAN MILES
T.T. Club

Remembering the first Lions Club TV Auction in 1973

Ron Kerney demonstrated his auctioneering style with a '67 Chev Belair, one of dozens of items that were auctioned off at the first Lions Club TV event in 1973. The car, donated by Katila Chev, was the top item in that first TV Auction and it fetched $525 for the AV Lions Club.

The first one, on December 1, 1973, was so successful the Alberni Valley Lions Club has held a TV Auction every year since. "Fantastic! It was way more than we expected," was the way Ron Kerney, then chairman of the auction committee described the event. "We had 10 phones set up to receive bids and they were swamped all night."

When the nine-hour broadcast was all said and done, the Lions Club had raised a total of $4,000 for charity.

"We sold Staff Sergeant Howie Turner's necktie for $32.50," Kerney marveled. "Even the kids got in on the act. A little girl offered her 89-cent ballpoint pen for auction and someone grabbed it for $11."

A 60-man auction crew started setting up in the Eighth Avenue School auditorium at 9am the day before for the big show.

"Everyone concerned was really terrific, the merchants (who donated all the major items), the Alberni TV crew, the school board and the public," Kerney added. "It was just wonderful the way everyone in the Valley responded to make the auction such a success."

Salute to Alberni Valley Lions Club's 55 years of service continues

The Alberni Valley Lions Club was "born" on September 24, 1955, and since then, its many members have always been active in the community. I don't think there has ever been a project that they haven't taken on, and I am sure the Club has supported just about every local cause or need that has come their way. So, from now until September, as a salute to more than five decades of "we serve", I am highlighting different Lions Club members and the memories they have created over the years.

Remember the Lions "Thankful Tankful" campaign? Local Lions Club members joined other clubs around the province filling tanks at participating Esso stations during Timmy's Telethon on December 3 and 4, 1988. As you may recall, proceeds from the telethon went to the B.C. Lions Society for Crippled Children. One cent from every litre pumped that weekend was donated to the telethon, and Imperial Oil Limited matched that total.
The AV Lions Club invaded Mick Earthy's Johnston Road Esso 22 years ago for the ninth annual Thankful Tankful event.
Shown above are: Esso representatives Mick Earthy and Dave McArthur, centre, and Lions members, left to right, Brett Lamontagne, Paul Dore and David Murray.

Port Alberni Mayor Jim Robertson signs a proclamation declaring Thursday, October 7, 1981, as "World Lions Service Day" while AV Lions Club representative Bob Critchley looks on. Local Lions distributed fresh fruit to needy senior citizens that day, joining fellow Lions around the world in providing services to the community.

It was July 30, 1975 when the local Family Guidance Association, received a $1,000 donation from the Alberni Valley Lions Club. Lions Denis Houle, left and Jim Rezac, right, presented the cheque to Helen Patenaude, second from left, and Shirley Luchinski, of the association.

Jim Robson's Alberni Valley Memories

Ike's Note

Long before I ever heard of CJAV and Port Alberni, I "met" Jim Robson. It was in the late fifties and Jim was broadcasting Vancouver Mounties baseball on CKWX. At that time, I had no idea that a decade later (1967), I would be starting my broadcasting career at the same radio station that Jim did in 1952. I first shook hands with "the voice" in the mid seventies when the late Bill Gibson introduced me to Jim in Vancouver. Of course, I met Jim again when he came back here in 1985 to celebrate the 30th anniversary of the Alberni Athletics winning the Canadian Basketball Championship. Now, I am looking forward, along with hundreds of others, to having dinner with Jim Robson on Friday, May 7 at the Multiplex. Jim has kindly agreed to be the keynote speaker for the Alberni Athletic Association's fundraiser – the Sportsmen's Dinner – with proceeds going to building the new Athletic Hall (some tickets may still be available by calling 250-723-7446.)

I asked Jim to send me a few notes of his time in the Alberni Valley (1952-56) and he kindly obliged. It is with great pleasure now that I can share with you .....

I started my first job in broadcasting at CJAV Port Alberni on July 1, 1952. I was 17, no experience, no training, but station manager Ken Hutcheson gave me a job - and paid me $100 per month. Seventy dollars out of that went to my "landlady", Mrs. Olive Wilson, on 2nd Avenue South, just above the Assembly Wharf.

My initial job at CJAV was writing commercials, greatly aided by 16-year old Doris Jowsey, who was actually in charge of the Continuity Dept.

Popular Bob Hall had just left the station to move "up" to CHWK Chilliwack, so the sportscasting work was available – and being a sports nut – the station said, "go ahead and do the sports". That meant doing play-by-play basketball, the red-hot sport of the time in the Albernis. Phil Barter and I worked together on the hoop broadcasts. Our first game was in October of 1952 – Alberni hosting Nanaimo Senior B's.

Harry Kermode was the playing-coach of that fine Alberni team and the leading scorer was a smooth guard from Vancouver named Al Brown. That team won 15 of 27 games but lost a playoff series to Victoria 3 games to 1.

The next year, Alberni mayor and super recruiter Fred Bishop brought in a former Seattle University stalwart named Elmer Speidel to be the A's player-coach. He turned out to be the perfect man for the job, an outstanding player and leader, and a man who fitted right in to the community. And yes, he's still here.

"Spider" brought in his jump shot and fast-break offence as the Athletics won 24 of 41 games. Speidel led the way, averaging 15 points per game in the era before the 'shot clock'. Bishop also brought in Doug Brinham from Ladysmith to join a solid group of "locals" – and the Alberni Athletics were on their way to fame.

The 1954-55 season saw additions like Rob Bissett and John Kootnikoff and the whole group combined to average 76 points per game and win 34 and lost only 10. They scored playoff series wins over Victoria, Vancouver Cloveleafs (in a most memorable seven game series), Edmonton and swept Sault Ste. Marie to win the Canadian Championship. That was when a National Senior Men's basketball title was front-page news.

The "old" Alberni Athletic Hall, the one that preceded the one recently destroyed by fire, was packed to the rafters for every game. Vic Simmons of Vic's Men's Wear on Victoria Quay was in charge of ticket sales and most were sold for the entire season.

I got to broadcast the games for four years, including that 1955 championship. The night the A's won the title, a "shut-in" in a wheelchair, Mrs. Spencer, presented me with a classy Rolex watch engraved "To Jim from the Fans". The watch is not running these days, but of course, I still have it.

Jim Robson in September 1952 at CJAV Port Alberni "This was my first job in broadcasting, I was 17."

My four years in the Albernis were extremely happy ones for me. I met many wonderful people, including my wife Bea, who was nursing at the West Coast General. I never caught a Tyee, never climbed Mount Arrowsmith, never saw Della Falls, but I tried all the sports – excelling in none.

I pitched some for the Port Alberni Cubs baseball team and surrendered one of the longest home runs ever hit at Stirling Field, as Doug Myles hit one into Kitsucksis Creek. I jumped to the Alberni A's ball team to join a winner, but the team was so good I sat on the bench. But there a man named Ted Okranitz told me that his brother-in-law was looking for an assistant. That would be Bill Stephenson, sports director of CKWX in Vancouver. I applied for the job, Bill hired me in the fall of 1956 – and my career took off.

But I'll never forget where it started, at "CJAV – 1240 on your dial – the Friendly Voice of the Alberni Valley".

"I retired on June 8, 1999, after 47 years in broadcasting," Jim noted.

That '70's Show...

The '70's are popular on TV right now, so I thought we'd go back there this time. Out of my personal archives(my wife calls me a pack rat of the past)and the memory bank, comes a few choice looks at what was the "decade of my life." More about me later....

First..."fire" caught the '70's local headlines twice in a big way. Who can forget the million dollar blaze that destroyed the Barclay Hotel on Christmas day 1976. Then, four days short of a year later, on Tuesday, December 20, 1977, Buffie's Auto Service, at 3rd and Kingsway was leveled by flames.

Other local history buffs will be quick to point out another flammable headline, all-be-it not as big as the other two, and that was the Hunter's Store fire, the first time in North America that a Martin Mars Water Bomber was used to douse a residential area blaze. It was in the hot Summer of 1973, when the historic landmark on the main highway, just past the former Sproat Elementary School, disappeared in a raging inferno.

There was plenty of good news too. In 1971, Premier W. A. C. Bennett visited Port Alberni to officially open the Seniors "High Rise" Pioneer Towers. A year earlier, a new Super Valu store opened in the brand new North Port plaza(now the home of buy-low foods). CJAV Radio changed hands in 1972, with Bill Gibson and Maurice Inwards taking over from Ken Hutcheson, and remember Bill and Mo going to press with the Barkley Sounder? The new Alberni Valley Museum was declared officially open, by deputy provincial secretary Laurie Wallace, on May 7, 1973.

Also in '73, the Clutesi Haven Marina was opened, and one year later, the Port Alberni Harbour Commission announced plans for a $500,000 marina expansion at China Creek. All local boaters and anglers can recall Gilbert Dore's 1973 Salmon Festival winning catch of 52.2 pounds. No one would beat that "big un" until Art Berlinski many years later, however, Jim MacDonald came close at 50.13 pounds in 1977.

In 1974, Ken Parke had expanded his Toyota Dealership at 3rd and Redford. He went from 8 new vehicles and one employee a few years before, to 30 new units in stock, 12 employees and a modern new showroom.

Across town, Neale Pennington's Chatwin Motors was also carrying a full line of Security recreational vehicles. BC Tel was completing the microwave installation project linking Port Alberni with Nanaimo, through Mt. Horne, at a cost of $766,000.

This scene of the Buffie's fire was captured by Roy Snikkers.

AND WHO CAN FORGET the drive by the Arrowsmith Ski Club to raise $150,000 to put a chair lift on our mountain. Of course the 70's ended with the opening of the Alberni Mall in April of 1979, and who could have predicted that 25 years later, a "power mall" would be located across the street. But at the time nobody could have guessed how economically devastating the 80's would be.

For me, the 70's gave me a bride, three beautiful children and a ton of lifelong memories. I hope the decade was good for you too. Hey, the class of '74 is having a reunion this year, more about that next time.

Ike Patterson has lived in the Alberni Valley for most of his life, more than 28 of those years "on the air" at CJAV, where as a young broadcaster he earned the nick name "Old Ike." He dug into the local radio station's past and along the way developed a keen interest in the Valley's colourful history. "The past is a present we can give to the future," Ike believes. He can be reached through the Pennyworth or e-mail lip.inc@shaw.ca

BILL GIBSON — MOE INWARDS — N.M. (Butch) BUCHKOWSKY — MIKE KETTERINGHAM
SHER GEYSON — BERNADETTE BJORNSON — MIKE KEETCH — IKE PATTERSON
HARRY DYLER — CAROL BOXRUD — CHRISTINE ANDREWS

Recognize any of these faces behind the pages of the 1973 Barkley Sounder?

More Fall Fair memories – from 1974

Murray Hole of Nanaimo is seen here about to drive home in the new Dodge Colt he won at the 1974 Fall Fair. He came back on Sept. 10 with his wife Eva and daughters June and Diane to take delivery of his $4,000 prize.

"The 29th annual Alberni District Fall Fair reached a record high paid attendance of 13, 288 and proved to be the biggest and best yet," was the lead line in the AV Times follow-up story on Monday, Sept. 9, 1974. If you were at the three-day event, you probably recall a Nanaimo man, Murray Hole, took home the top prize, the Fall Fair car. A Port Alberni mill worker's wife, Mrs. Diane Lupichuk, won the Kinsmen's $1,000 cash draw.

A Campbell River man, J. McCormick won his choice of a trip to Hawaii or $1,000 cash in the Chinese Tea Garden draw. John Peterson of Port Alberni got lucky in the Shriner's Draw and won a $1,200 colour TV set, and included in the many other draws, a local 12-year old Boy Scout, Wayne Machan, won the burl table raffled off by the Junior Hospital Auxiliary.

Diane Lupichuk of Port Alberni shows off the one thousand dollar bill she won at the Fair. With her at the presentation ceremonies at the Kin hut on the Tuesday after the event were: husband Ken and baby Kalvin, Trina, Kevin and Faith.

Were you at ADSS on November 17, 1969? Then you'd recall the new school cafeteria

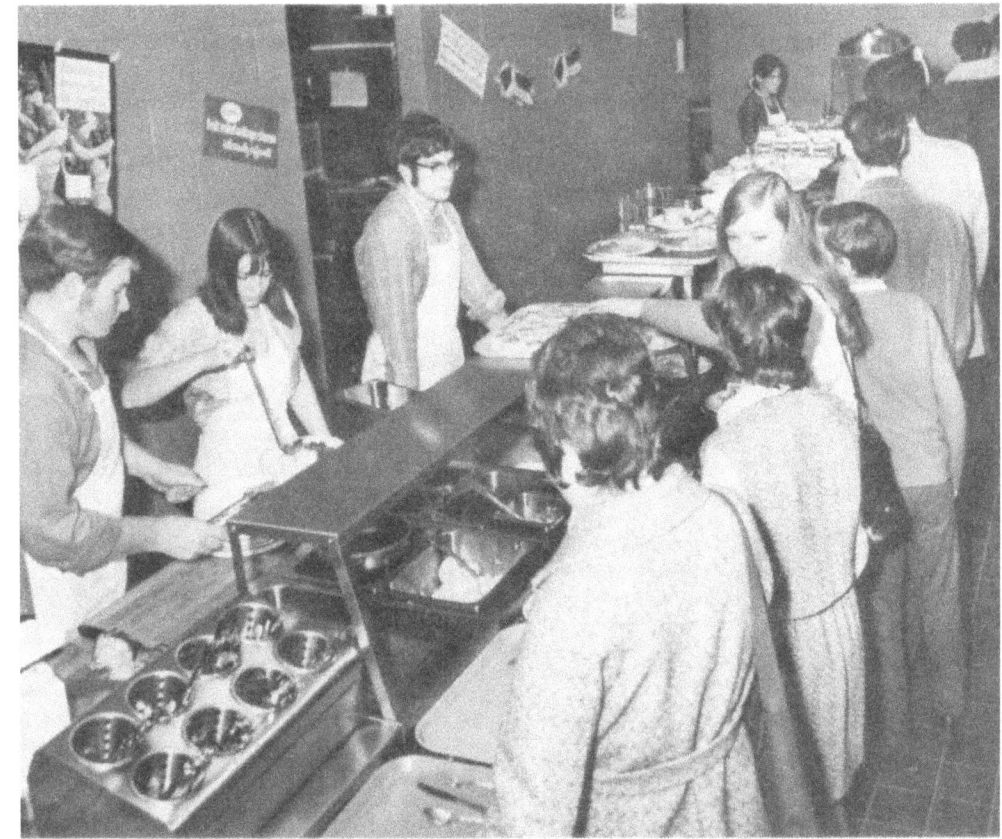

You may be in one of these pictures (from the 1970 ADSS year book) taken when the cafeteria opened in the Community Services Wing at the high school 41 years ago.

"Students and teachers flocked to the open doors to partake of gourmet foods with prices that even a teacher can afford," is how the write-up read in the 1970-year book. "We give our thanks to Mr. Bauer and the Foods 12 classes for their diligent work, organization and well prepared meals."

By the way, you're bound to see many of your former classmates in town on August 27 and 28 as the class of 1970 holds a 40-year reunion at the Italian Hall. If you have not been contacted, or if you still haven't registered, call the reunion committee right away. Cecilia at 250-724-6806 and Marilyn at 250-244-1949 are the contacts.

NOW THIS IS A STORY THAT REFUSES TO GO AWAY...

Just when you think you've heard everything there was to know about Paul Hertel's unusual "Zoo" out in Beaver Creek, someone else brings in a memory to share.

Margaret Bowen (nee Germain) found these two pictures among her mother's things. Both snapshots have "1956" written on them and Margaret said her brother "Harold" was born in 1948, so that would be about right.

After listening to quite a few people on this subject – some willing to take a lie detector test – I have come to believe the Zoo was out at Hertel's property on Bland Road until 1957 (open to the public in '54), then was moved to Nanaimo, near Rutherford Mall, where it stayed open for a few years.

The Zoo was closed down a short time after a tragic accident when one of lions got out and killed a little girl. Details are still sketchy as to exactly when the facility stopped operating and what happened to all of the animals.

Also, some neighbours insist the cougars were found, not purchased or adopted, as reported by out of town newspapers in late 1953. And they say Paul had Hans & Fritz in 1948, not early in 1953 as quoted in the Daily Colonist article on Dec. 18, 1953.

That's Harold Germain with one of Paul Hertel's cougars. It was taken out Beaver Creek at the Zoo, fifty years ago. Margaret said whoever snapped the picture accidentally cut off the heads, but that's Paul with his shirt off on the right, and she thinks that the gentleman on the left was a relative visiting from the prairies, at the time.

For those who were not here prior to November 14, 1948, this photo clearly shows how formidable "Angel Rock" appeared. It is believed that Joseph Clegg, who passed away in 1961, took this picture in the late 1930's. Thanks to Cecile Kropninski for making it available for all of us to see.

CHRISTMAS DAY 1976 – THE BARCLAY HOTEL DESTROYED IN AN EARLY MORNING FIRE

This photo was taken soon after the old Barclay Pacific Hotel was opened on March 1st, 1957. For those of you who weren't here then, the Hotel was located on Third Avenue (where Haggard Trucking is now). It was back from the sidewalk a little further as you can see in the picture. Rooms went for six dollars a night then.

The second picture (courtesy of the P.A. Fire Department), was taken when the fire was out of control. News reports at the time recorded that that fire department fought the blaze for four hours after receiving the initial call at 1:10am.

The bottom picture (also from the P.A. Fire Dept), shows the still smoldering ruins after day break. I remember being on the scene at first light, reporting for CJAV. Later, Steve Laschuk, the majority shareholder, said the Hotel was considered a total write-off by insurance underwriters and the replacement cost was estimated at $2 million

After the blaze, the owners, Lashchuk and his two partners, Carl Poznikoff and Corey Porter, Laschuk's brother-in-law, said they hoped to begin re-building within the next two months.

However, things don't always go as planned. It took the partners almost four years to bring the popular hotel back.

When it did return, opening on November 15th, 1980, it was as the Barclay Pacific Rodeway Inn, a first class hotel costing between 4 and 5 million dollars to complete.

Not only was the Barclay a brand new facility, the likes of which the Valley had never seen before, it was at a new location, the corner of Stamp & Roger.

A lot has happened in the local accommodation business since that Christmas morning 30 years ago, when we lost the old Barclay, but that's another story!

THIS IS WHAT THUNDER IN THE VALLEY LOOKED LIKE 48 YEARS AGO

Remembering Ray Bowerman's "Candy Apple Roadster," alias the "Century Stormer."

Ray Bowerman was 21 years old when this picture was taken in 1958, near the Skipsey house, at the corner of Princess and Leslie.

It's a "gear head's" dream weekend coming up - a Show 'n' Shine this Friday at the Harbour Quay, then the 1/4 Mile Drag Races at the Airport this Saturday and Sunday. But Drag Racing isn't new to Valley "Quarter Milers," just ask Ray Bowerman, who owned a "32 Ford Roadster" that he used to race down on the entrance road to the Bamberton Cement plant in 1958.

"That was about the only place on the Island you could do a quarter mile drag back then," Ray recalled. "I used to enter the local hill climbs up the old hump road too." The "Candy Apple Roadster," aptly named for it's "hey look at me paint job," was also nick-named the "Century Stormer" because of the 1956 Buick Century motor. "It was 322 cubic inches, but after certain additions and modifications, it could put out about 300 hp," Ray told me last Saturday. "When I bought the car the owners, Chuck and Wimpy Robinson, were racing it in Abbotsford."

Ray sold the Ford, to someone in the Interior in 1961, however, he believes a local fellow rescued it years later, bringing it back home, where some pieces may still be around. I called Wayne Earthy, who remembers Ray's '32 Ford "as being the top car in town at the time." Wayne, Barry Thompson and Cliff West were among the locals who raced at Bamberton along with Ray.

BY THE WAY...

It should be mentioned that efforts to come up with a "drag strip and club house building site" started officially back in May, 1955, when the "Albernis Auto Club" was formed. According to newspaper reports of the day, Eddie Not was chosen President, with Jim Mar vice-president, Jack Fix, secretary and Eddie Erickson, treasurer. Jack Fraser, Glen Pakenham and David Willis were named directors. What do you recall about "Ray's Roadster?"

RECOGNIZE ANYONE IN THIS PICTURE?

Terry Neyedli's father, Joe, is in this photo of shingle sawyers, weavers and packers (first on the left in the second row).

"I believe the picture was taken by Charnell Studios sometime between 1955-58," Terry mentioned when he brought it in this week. "My dad worked at the Somass until the early '70's. The shingles in the picture are 'number one", which is the top grade and they were shipped all over the world."

Terry knows a couple of others in the photo; like Ches Dockendorff (first on the left in the back row) and Norm Johnson (third from the right in the second row).

A LOOK BACK AT THE THREE SISTERS CAFE!

WOW! WHAT A RESPONSE TO LAST WEEK'S TRAIN PHOTO!

First of all, that picture was taken at Franklin River and thanks to a number of people, we now know quite a bit more about it and the whole Franklin River operation. For example, information that has come in now verifies that the photo was taken sometime after the #19 was delivered to Bloedel, Stewart & Welch from Seattle where it was purchased in December of 1940. We also know that it is indeed Camp B in the background – the first Camp B – established in 1936, at Corrigan Creek. Thanks to former Franklin River resident and employee, Don Watt (his dad Jack worked at Franklin River from 1936 to 1971), we also know that the picture had to have been taken before the second Camp B was opened at Parson's Creek in 1942-43. See Don's story and photos on page 18 and check the comments from readers below.

Ray Barron, who has a model railroad operation in his back yard, was the first to respond to the picture of "number 19". He brought in information confirming that Bloedel, Stewart & Welch Ltd. bought the Pacific Coast class Shay in 1940. Number 19 (manufacturer's # 3352) was the second last Shay ever manufactured and it was built in 1938 by Lima Locomotive Works in Lima, Ohio, which had been in business since the turn of the century. The 3-truck, 90 ton Shay became No. 1019 when MacMillan merged with B.S.& W. in 1952 and was scrapped in 1959. Wayne Ruttan then emailed about the picture saying it couldn't have been Franklin River Camp B, which is 14 miles by the old road from Port.

"I believe this to be probably the one before branch 25," he wrote. "I came to work at Camp 9 (Great Central Lake) in 1945."
Although Curly never worked in Camp B itself, he did log in various other locations over the years and he still recalls much of what went on, especially in the 40's and 50's. I am hoping to have more with him in future columns.
Clara Hill (nee Levander), who spent part of her childhood at the first Camp B in the picture, was able to shine even more light on the situation.

"The building on the top right was the schoolhouse," she told me. "I was 7 years old when we moved to Camp B in 1937. There were 11 kids, in all grades, in that one-room schoolhouse. The buildings on the left are some of the "family houses". I remember there were about ten of those homes. In front of the locomotive (out of the picture) there were bunkhouses, a cookhouse, even a 'volleyball type of court'. We had woodstoves, running water and power, but it was shut off each night at 10pm."
Clara said her family lived at the first Camp B for about three years, and then went to Camp A before going on to the second Camp B. They moved to Port Alberni in 1943 or 1944.

And, Ken Rutherford, a well-known train aficionado emailed last Saturday, confirming the history of the number 19 that Ray Barron had brought in earlier.
"I liked the picture of the locomotive at Camp B," he mentioned. "Of note, BS&W had the largest stable of Pacific Coast Shays of any logging operation in North America."
Ken correctly added that #19 was the last 90-ton Shay ever built, but according to Ray Barron's information, the last Shay ever made was a 150-ton monster built in 1945 for the Western Maryland. Railway.

FRANKLIN RIVER'S "CAMP B" EXPLAINED!!
Thanks to details and pictures from Don Watt

Franklin River's Camp B had three locations over the years. The first one (in last week's photo of the number 19 locomotive) was at Corrigan Creek.

"My dad, Jack Watt, was transferred from Great Central Lake to what they called Franklin Creek when it opened in 1936," Don Watt said last Saturday as he brought me up to speed on Franklin River. "Our family moved to the second Camp B at Parsons Creek in the fall of 1943 and then on to the third Camp B located at Coleman Creek in 1946."

Don, who was born in 1939, grew up in Franklin River and started working there in 1957.

"I left for awhile, came back in 1961 and stayed until taking early retirement in 1998," he said. "My son Mike also worked there for a number of years."

Don also has information that shows Number 19 was indeed built in June 1938, sold to BS&W in January 1940 and scrapped in 1959.

"That would confirm that the photo from last week, at the Corrigan Creek Camp B, was most likely taken within the two year span between spring 1940 to early 1942 when Camp B was moved to the Parsons Creek site," Don added.

The picture above is a "night shot" of Camp B at Corrigan Creek, taken in 1938. You can see the schoolhouse on the hill, on the right, and the married houses on the left. Yes, Clara Hill, it looks like there were ten houses to me.

This aerial shot of the third and final location of Camp B at Coleman Creek was taken in 1950.

"Our house was #135 and it was 8th from the left in the second row," Don pointed out. "Folks should be able to spot the cookhouse, rec centre, school and the house where Jack Bell, the general foreman, lived."

I'll have more on life at the third and final Camp B site (Coleman Creek), the one most people recall, next week. And, did you know there was a "Camp C" at Franklin River?

BARLOW'S HOME ENTERTAINMENT CENTRE – BORN IN 1969!

This picture shows Ken (on the right) and Keith (middle) delivering brand new TV sets to Alec Simmons at the King Edward Hotel in 1970.

It has been almost 40 years since Ken Barlow and Keith Adams started what has literally become a living legend among retailers in the Alberni Valley. Barlow's Home Entertainment Centre has stood the test of time and the onslaught of outside competition for so long most residents feel as though the store has always been on Lower Third Avenue.

Keith left the business in 1974 (and later opened the Port Light House), while Ken and his staff has continued to provide the best possible value and service anywhere around, from the same location.

How High Was The Water???

Most people know the story of the Clutesi Haven Marina, which was opened in 1973. Part of the Marina occupies what was Arrowsmith Engineering, one of the many businesses damaged during the 1964 Tidal Wave. In the photo on the left, Jack Butterworth, then owner of Arrowsmith Engineering, points to the "high water" mark (48 1/2 inches) on the building which suffered thousands of dollars damage to the interior. The photo on the right shows former mayors Les Hammer and Fred Bishop commemorating the "high water level" with a special plague during the opening ceremonies 9 years later. That special plaque is still on the Marina building today. More on the Clutesi Haven Marina in weeks to come.

Photo courtesy of May Lueke

Photo taken by Roy Snikkers

Did You Know??? The first Port Alberni High School opened in 1913 on 12th Avenue. (where the old Calgary school used to be, just down from KFC) High School students were moved down to 5th & Redford (where the now closed Redford school is)then moved up the former Army Camp (the Glenwood Centre area) before settling in to the brand new ADHS in 1951(now known as ADSS of course)

Rare photo shows legendary Alberni Athletics "victory cheer"
After they won the Canadian Senior Men's Basketball Championships on April 16, 1955

Fifty-five years ago, the Alberni Valley became the "Basketball Capitol of Canada" when the Alberni Athletics dumped the Sault St. Marie Gunners in three straight games to grab the Canadian Men's Basketball Championship.

Much has been said, written – and discussed– over the years about the night of April 16, 1955. That championship win, in the original Alberni Athletic Hall, lead the way to a massive community effort to build a new, regulation-size facility, which opened in January 1958. That was the hall lost in a fire last May and the reason another concerted community effort is underway right now – to BUILD A NEW ALBERNI ATHLETIC HALL! The famous "can do" thinking of over half a century ago, has resurfaced among Valley residents, former residents and those who have attended functions in the Athletic Hall over the last 51 years.

That Port Alberni "lets get it done" train of thought has paved the way for the new Athletic Hall to be built far from the previous two buildings on Beaver Creek Road (and the floodplain) to up between the Multiplex and North Island College. This site will be the scene of much activity over the coming months as the building develops, but for now, the fundraising continues.

That brings us back to 1955, because some of those Alberni Athletic players on that championship team will be at the Association's "Sportsmen's Dinner", an unprecedented fundraising event on May 7 at the Multiplex.

"Seven of the original thirteen players from the '55 team will be at the dinner," Denny Grisdale advised. "And, at least seven of the original 13 players from the 1965 championship team will be on hand."

Hockey Hall of Fame Broadcaster Jim Robson, who was the voice of the Athletics on CJAV back then, will be the keynote speaker on May 7.

"I still have the beautiful watch given to me by listeners on April 16, 1955," Jim told me recently. "It doesn't run now, but it sure brings back a lot of memories."

Reports in the West Coast Advocate following the big win said:

"Only person at a loss for words during the evening was CJAV's Jim Robson, who was struck speechless when presented with a watch on behalf of the shut-ins among his basketball broadcast listeners. Mrs. Beatrice Spencer, an arthritic, presented the beautiful wrist-chronometer to Robson."

Former BCTV sports broadcaster, John McKeachie, will also be taking to the podium during the upcoming fun evening of food and memories, which will be emceed by Evan Hammond of The Peak, as CJAV is called today.

Former City Councillor and the arena voice of the Alberni Valley Bulldogs, Charles Mealey, will be on the microphone during the silent and live auctions.

Tickets are $100 per person (tax receipts are available upon request) at Somass Drugs, Barlow's, Watson's Paint and Echo Centre. For more ticket information and table reservations, contact Vicky Seredick at 250-723-7446.

Remember the past – and be part of the future – while supporting the new Alberni Athletic Hall fundraising campaign. Come for a dinner of a lifetime on Friday, May 7.

This seldom-seen picture was in a package of articles given to me by a "This Was Then" fan years ago. I contacted Denny Grisdale, who is in the photo, for help in identifying the others.

"Anton Snikkers took this picture just after we won the final game," Denny pointed out. "That's Elmer Speidel, our playing coach, in the center of the picture," Denny pointed out. "Going clockwise from him is Roy Durante, our trainer, then Ron Bissett, John Kootnekoff, Joe Buchanan, Laurie Veitch, Joe Samarin, John Groholski, Doug Brinham and Al Brown (partially hidden behind team manager Fred Bishop), Fred, Denny and off to the right, John Williamson, president of the Alberni Athletic Association."

Proof that the big ones were out there – in 1982

The late Charlie Haggard was a big guy. That's why the 63-pounder that he was holding in 1982 looks like an anchovy.

"The monster met its doom at Haggard's hands at San Mateo Bay," the caption under this picture read when it appeared in the A.V. Times on Monday, September 27, 1982.

Too bad for Charlie that he caught it after the Salmon Festival 27 years ago – that was the one that Art Berlinski won with a 60 pound, eight-ounce Chinook (still the largest fish weighed in since the Festival started back in 1972).

When did we become the Salmon Capital of the World?

City Council formally adopted the 'Salmon Capitol of the World' designation as the city motto on Monday, September 13, 1982.

Bob Cole, the 1982 Salmon Festival co-ordinator, provided some impressive figures to back up our right to snatch the title from Campbell River.

"There were 18,901.89 pounds of fish caught," he reported. "The total represents the combined weight of 1,346 fish caught by the 3,600 entrants."

In 1981, 3,500 fishermen caught 1,133 fish weighing in at a total of 14,435 pounds.

"Port Alberni is the Salmon Capitol of the World and that title will stay here as long as there is federal money in the Robertson Creek Hatchery," remarked Charlie Haggard, then of Quality Sports, on October 1, 1982.

Remember the "braggin buttons" that came out in 1982? Local artist Rick Dupont created the logo and JAL Signs and Designs provided the marketing expertise so that we could flaunt our new status.

KEN BARLOW ON AMALGAMATION 40 YEARS LATER!

"I think it was the best thing to ever happen to Port Alberni," Ken reflected as he looked back at himself in a 1967 Amalgamation newspaper ad. "It was definitely the thing to do!"

Ken, who worked at Hollway Radio & Record Centre downtown, at the time of amalgamation, went on to open his own business in 1969, in the same location he's at today.

"People said we were going to starve to death on lower Third Avenue," Ken said with a chuckle. " Keith Adams and I started out together and then he went on to greater things and is now retired."

After 38 years, Ken is starting to take more time off to roam and play golf, while the staff at Barlow's takes up the slack.

"It's been a slice," he said. "Port Alberni has been just great to me, so no regrets."

"I WAS BORN ON AMALGAMATION DAY!"
Gidget McLeod shares her birthday with the City of Port Alberni!

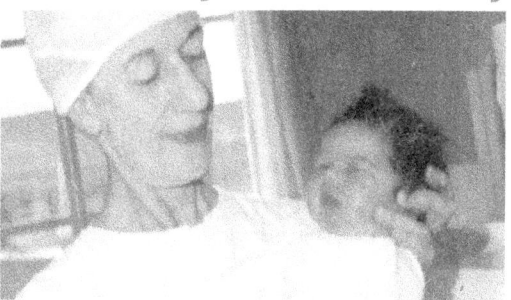

Gidget now – and then!

"I read that you were looking for pictures from the Amalgamation," Gidget commented when she arrived at the Pennyworth office recently. "So I came to see you."

"I'm a real Amalgamation Baby", Gidget McLeod told me recently, as she held out her birth certificate and this baby picture to show she was born on October 28, 1967 at West Coast General.

"I don't know the name of the nurse who is holding me," she confessed. "But the hospital records show that Gidget was born on October 28, 1967, at 5:42am, to Constant and Wayne McLeod. She weighted 9 pounds and 2 ounces.

"My family traveled a lot when I was growing up," Gidget revealed. "I returned about 3 years ago and I plan on staying here for a long time."

Welcome Home Gidget! Lordy! Lordy! Everyone knows you'll be "forty" real soon.

JACK SEYMOUR WAS AN ORIGINAL MEMBER OF THE ALBERNI VALLEY CENTENNIAL COMMITTEE

And he still has the "one hundred year Free Pass" to Echo Pool to prove it.

88 year-old Sidney J. Seymour (Jack) is one of the last surviving members of a small group of volunteers that we can thank for us enjoying Echo '67 Centre for the last 40 years.

"I'm glad I had sense enough to do something that has satisfied so many people over the years," Jack told me recently. "I sure am glad to see the amount of people using Echo Centre today. It's fantastic!"

Jack, who worked for the School District for 37 years, volunteered to be on the Committee that narrowed down the choices suggested for the Centennial Project.

All politics aside, Jack still recalls the slim 20-vote majority on May 28, 1966, that brought Echo Centre into being. It was the third time people had gone to the polls on the issue.

"People in Port Alberni didn't want to spend any more money," Jack revealed. "The present location of the pool/community centre was always our first choice, although there was talk about having the indoor pool near ADSS."

Jack was on hand for the sod-turning on January 9, 1967, the opening on October 27, 1967, and he plays crib there pretty well every week. Jack plans to be at Echo Centre on Saturday, October 27th for the 40th Anniversary Celebrations, after all he's still got 60 years left on his Free Pass. Thanks Jack!

This group picture of the Centennial Committee that Jack is holding, was taken in 1965 by Anton's Studios (Anton Snikkers)

Left to right-standing: Ronald Hess, Jim McFie, Bill Marshall, Armour Ford, Dunc Russell, Garnet Reynolds, Jack Seymour, and A.G.Cardinal.

Left to right-seated: Russ Foxcroft, Harry Shorter, Pauline M. Barrett, Bill Russell, Dorrit L. MacLeod, Bev Raikes and Jack Dunbar.

Absent when the picture was taken: Edna Souther, Edmond Chenard and Catherine Williamson.

The Honorary Members (not shown) were Mayor Les Hammer of Port Alberni, Mayor Fred Bishop of Alberni, Alderman George Cole, Capt. R.D. Barrett and Ken Hutcheson.

STORY BURIED BY AMALGAMATION CELEBRATIONS!

Lots of people have forgotten or didn't know about the 'time capsule' buried at the entrance to Echo '67 Centre on October 29, 1967.

Thousands of folks have gone by the plaque outside of Echo Centre's main entrance thousands of times in the last 40 years. Most have never noticed that a 'time capsule' is buried beneath the welcoming words written by Pauline M. Barrett and presented by The Alberni Valley Chamber of Commerce in 1967.

The October 21, 1967 issue of the Nanaimo Daily Free Press carried a story and the pictures above, under the header "Open in 2067." The caption read, in part:

"Items of historical interest have been chosen for the capsule, donated by MacMillan and Bloedel, so that citizens 100 years from now will get a look at life at the end of Canada's first century. Members of the project, from left to right: Dick Christie, Jack Goldie, George Guy and Keith Rodgers."

Just what is inside the capsule – is in doubt now – but according to Ken Hutcheson, then Chairman of the Centennial Amalgamation Celebrations Committee, "There is a reel-to-reel tape made by CJAV and a newspaper of the day."

'A couple of odd coins and some newspaper items is about all I can remember being in the capsule," Jack Goldie told me recently. "I made it and George Guy welded it. We put the stuff in and then we took it to the instrument department and they took all the air out of it."

Were you at the special ceremony at Echo '67 Centre at 2pm on Sunday, October 29th, 1967 when then MLA Dr. H.R. McDiarmid buried the capsule.

ECHO CENTRE CARRIES HER NAME!

It was Jane Hanson (now Kruks) who suggested the name "Echo '67 Centre" 40 years ago. Jane, a Grade 5 student at Wood School then, won $100 for her suggestion, which was selected out of over 2,000 entries from students in local schools.

"I thought it was a prank at first," Jane, recalled when she first heard that she had won. "When Mr. Russell (Bill Russell) came to the school with the prize I was flabbergasted!"

And what ever happened to the one hundred dollars?

"My parents were so pleased they allowed me spend it all," Jane told me recently. "I bought Christmas presents for my family and for myself - some Nancy Drew books, ice skates and a charm bracelet."

Although "the '67" was dropped from the name over the years, Jane's suggestion ("I thought of how your voice echoes when you call a friend in the pool," she revealed.), has stood the test of time and "Echo Centre" itself has more than lived up to the needs of the Community, proving that it was the perfect choice for a Centennial project in 1967.

Today, Jane continues her winning way with words, as a School District 70 teacher, who presently has the privilege of working in various schools in the area of her passion – literacy!

Monday, march 1st, 1948 - Woodward's Opens

The below information was taken from an article in the March 14, 1948 edition of *Island Events*

WOODWARD'S GOING AHEAD WITH THE ALBERNIS

Opening of New Department Store in Port Alberni Signifies Faith in Future Development of West Coast District

Photo by Sparshatt & Barr
On the main floor are fashions, ladies' wear, draperies, shoes, notions, stationery, drugs and men's and boys' clothing.

JOHN KENNETH WHYTE
General Manager

Men's clothing section carries a smart selection of suits and topcoats in addition to shirts, underwear, shoes and other men's clothing.

Photo by Sparshatt and Barr
Above photos give some idea of the spacious food department of Woodward's in Port Alberni. Woodward's now have stores in Vancouver, Port Alberni and Edmonton.

FRUIT AND VEGETABLE SECTION OF the food floor is a model of perfection. At the right Bill Latimer, manager of Woodward's grocery section, weighs some vegetables.

Friday, June 25th, 1993 - Last day for Woodward's!

The historic Port Alberni store closed at 9 pm – reopened as Zellers in mid September.

This group shot of the Woodward's staff was taken in mid-June 1993, just before the store closed forever. You're bound to recognize quite a few of the former employees, as Bob Casault did when he saw the picture (first on the left in the front row).

"I still have that tie," Bob exclaimed. "Pat McKelvey, sitting in the middle of the front row, was the last Store Manager in Port Alberni. Roy Vance is standing right behind me and Betty Norris is behind him."

I also showed the picture to Albert Laslo, who worked at Woodward's for over 30 years but left in 1991.

"I know the first name of pretty well everyone shown," he said as he pointed to Bev, Lodi, and Tara. "Ted Blight, standing directly behind Pat, was another long-time employee at Woodward's."

When you see yourself, email your thoughts about what it was like to have been one of the last to work at the famous 3rd Avenue store.

Actually, I would also like to hear from any of the hundreds of other folks who took home a pay cheque from Woodward's, undoubtedly one of the most influential businesses this Valley has ever seen.

Time had already run out for Woodward's Department Store when the sign came down in September 1993.

Royal Visit among Valley's big stories in 1951

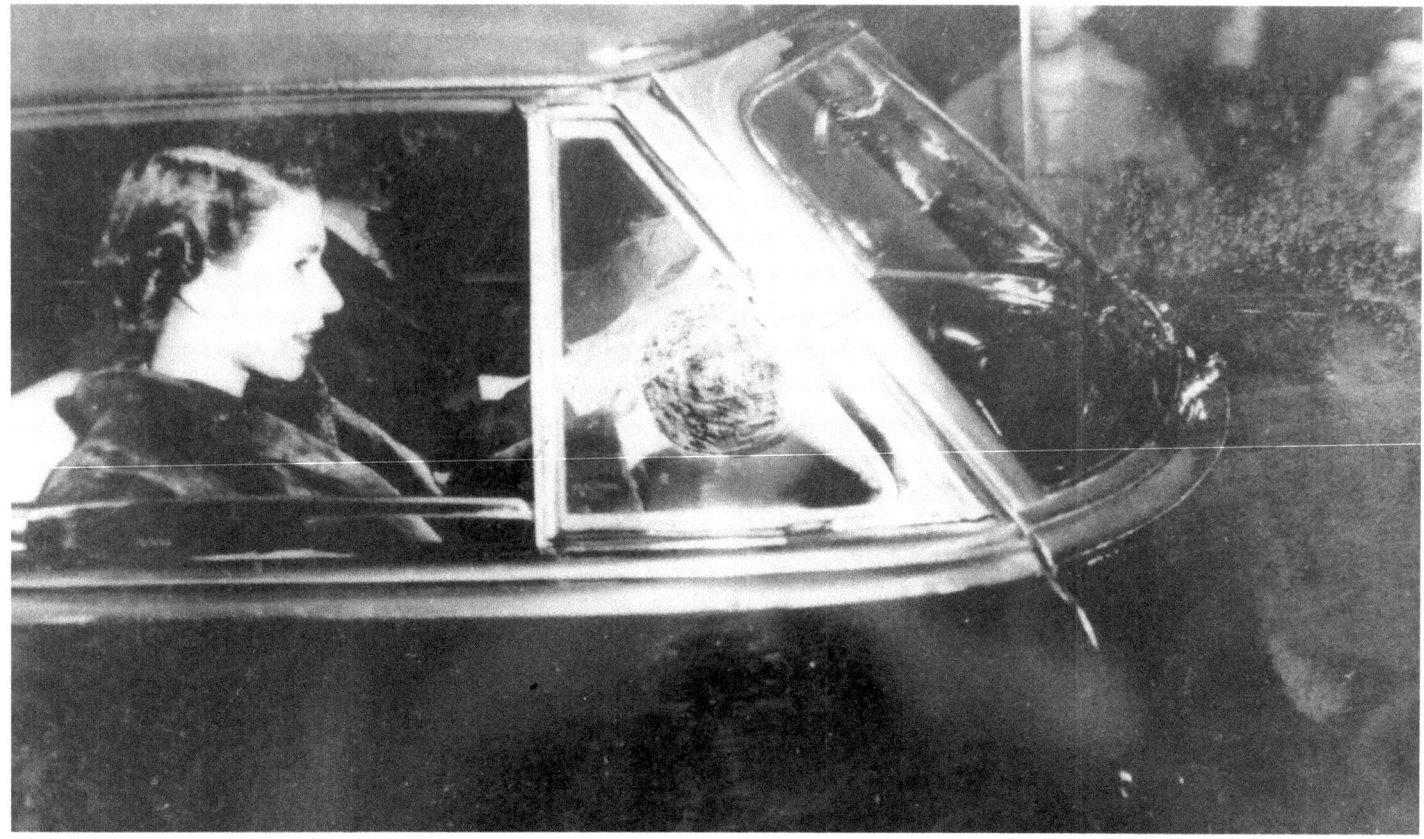

This picture of Princess Elizabeth taken on October 25, 1951 as she passed by with Prince Philip on that surprise "drive-thru" visit to the Albernis comes from Fred Boyko Jr.'s personal photo collection.
"I can't recall who gave me the picture," Fred told me last Monday. "I think it was taken near Woodward's store. I was there and it was a nice day; the car windows were rolled down so everyone could see them. I remember they drove slowly but never actually stopped, but I can't recall if Prince Philip was driving."

"1951's biggest news event was written into the history of the Alberni Valley within two hours of the late afternoon of Thursday, October 25, when Princess Elizabeth and her consort, Prince Philip of Edinburgh, in response to several appeals from this district paid an unscheduled visit to the Twin Cities and environs."

That was how the article read in the West Coast Advocate on Thursday, December 27, 1951. The story was part of a year-end review in the weekly Advocate and it went on to report:

"If spontaneous reaction of the residents to the visit is taken as the criterion then the Royal Visit and twin cities streets drive was one of the biggest events in the history of the community. One thing is sure, it drew the largest turnout of residents. A close estimate of the throngs who flanked Johnston Road and Victoria Quay and Port Alberni's Stamp and Third Avenues was impossible but experienced observers of street crowds placed the minimum at 10,000."

Now, many people have told me over the years about how on the morning of Oct. 25, CJAV broadcast the fact that Princess Elizabeth and Prince Philip were going to pay a last-minute surprise visit to the Valley that afternoon, and how they were taken out of school to glimpse the Royal couple drive by. I've been told that Prince Philip was behind the wheel when they drove up Third Avenue, and turned around at Woodward's Store.

I've written about the Queen's visit (when she was still a Princess) before, but decided to clarify the date again because recently many people, who weren't here at the time, have been asking about when or if the event actually happened.

A Salmon Festival 'now and then' moment

The salmon barbecue served every year by the Port Alberni Kiwanis Club has always been a mainstay at the Labour Day Salmon Festival. This year was no exception, but it was also special because Art Wynans was back.

Art, who has been the grill master since the first Salmon Festival in 1972, was conspicuously absent in 2009. He was in hospital recovering from serious injuries suffered in a cycling accident.

However, last weekend when regulars and first-timers lined up to sample the delicious salmon, Art was there, applying the heat along with the Kiwanis Club's top-secret sauce recipe. His son Chris joined Art this year, something that also happened 29 years ago. So, as a welcome back tribute to Art Wynans, one of the original members of the Salmon Festival committee, and a long time "barbecue griller", this photo salute!

Now - Art and Chris back at the Kiwanis barbecue grill.

Then – Art and Chris at the 1981 Salmon Festival.

June 6, 1985 – The Alberni Valley became the "Community with a Heart"

On Thursday, June 6, 1985, the Alberni Valley received the "Community Heart Award" from Variety Club Tent 47 in Vancouver. The award was presented by Barker Aurla McGarvey and Chief Barker George Pitman during ceremonies at the Four Seasons Hotel. This was the first time the Community Heart Award was awarded and it was given for the "outstanding efforts and contributions of the people of the Alberni Valley."

A special plaque was received by Mayor Gillian Trumper and Joanne Melling, local Variety Club Telethon coordinator, on behalf of the Alberni Valley.

"This award is for all the wonderful people who have worked so hard to raise money in the Valley," Mayor Trumper said in thanking the organizers.

Other awards presented that night at the Variety Club's Annual Heart Awards dinner included the Eagle River Challenge Trophy, which went to the students of Cherry Creek Elementary School for their contribution to the Telethon. Dave Grant, principal, accepted the trophy from Barbara Stewart, a long-time Variety Club member.

"They think it is just wonderful," Dave remarked later when asked about the reaction of his students who raised more per capita than any other school in B.C. to parallel the charitable efforts in the Alberni Valley when it came to the Variety Club Telethon. Grant's kids raised $10.97 per student, or $2,182 to win the top spot for schools in the province.

"Community with a Heart" – it still suits us 25 years later! Thanks to those who earned it then and to everyone in the Valley who has continued to work so hard each year since for the Variety Club Telethon.

Mayor Gillian Trumper (second from right) receives the plaque naming Port Alberni and the surrounding Alberni Valley the community with the largest heart in B. C. Pictured with the mayor are (left to right) George Pitman, chief barker for Variety Club Tent 47; Aurla McGarvey, fund-raising chairman and Joanne Melling, Alberni coordinator for the Telethon.

"People are the most wonderful people......

Out of the mouth of a South Surrey Eagles fan...came the inspiration for this month's column. Last week I had a casual conversation with a lovely lady from Surrey at the Multiplex. She related how her father thoroughly enjoyed his Winter games visit to our Valley and insisted she try the Clam Bucket restaurant when she came to town. Her story about how they had to stay in Nanaimo each night(no room at the local inns)and her more than favorable impressions of the people here topped off my "community pride reserve", which tends to drop a little due to evaporation sometimes.

This woman's unsolicited approval of our town was so outpouring it took me back to the '90's when I was told by Robert Kennedy Junior that we lived in "one of the most desirable areas in the world". He was in Port Alberni as the special guest speaker at the 12th annual Nuu-Chah-Nulth Indian Games(as it was called then)

Forty years ago this weekend, a Tidal Wave hit the then communities of Alberni and Port Alberni. I've researched, talked and written about what was undoubtedly the most significant event to ever occur here(See Val Hughes column and Inside Our Museum on page 13 for more)

As most of you know I arrived in the Valley in 1967, just before the two towns amalgamated to become "the biggest new city on Vancouver Island". This amalgamation process actually started back in 1964, shortly after the Tsunami.

On another note** Let's go back 60 years to 1944. The year's top story: "D-Day in Normandy; Allied forces land on the beaches in Operation Overlord". The best movie was "Going My Way", the Montreal Canadiens beat Chicago to win the Stanley Cup, and the top tunes of the times included "You Always Hurt the One You Love", "Till Then" and "Swinging on a Star". I'm not old enough to remember, but bobby socks and penny loafers were the rage. Hey, anyone know if the class of '44 is getting together?

One from the "request line" so-to-speak. Knowing my fondness for music, a lady asked me recently if I knew what the worst rock n' roll single of all time was. Well, I looked it up, but I don't agree with the decision. "My Ding-a-Ling" by Chuck Berry. Send your requests to the Pennyworth, or leave a message at my home number 724-2234.

Robert Kennedy Junior, the famous environmental lawyer, being interviewed by Old Ike, during the 12th Annual Nuu-Chah-Nulth Indian Games in Port Alberni.

PORT ALBERNI & ALBERNI, B.C.
AMALGAMATION MEDAL

1791
Alberni Canal was named after Pedro Alberni, a Spanish Army Captain.
1860
Captain Stamp and Gilbert Sproat arrived to establish Anderson Sawmill.

1912
Port Alberni City incorporated under Mayor Waterhouse.
1913
Alberni City incorporated under Mayor C.F. Bishop.
1967
Twin Cities Amalgamate under Mayors
E.L. Hammer, Port Alberni
F.A. Bishop, Alberni

Ike's note

As most of you know this Christmas, and all others, will not be the same for my family and me. Although the loss of my wife, my children's mother and their children's' grandmother has taken most of the joy out of the season, I can never forget that Christmas was Linda's favourite time of the year. She literally infected everyone around with the Christmas spirit. Her decorating skills and love of snowmen were well known, as was her strong belief in the real meaning of Christmas. We both treasured the timeless tradition of exchanging greetings and good wishes with everyone, something I intend to continue, painful, as it may be this Holiday Season.

That said, as my way of wishing all This was Then readers a "Merry Christmas", I would like to pass along this editorial (author unknown) taken from the Twin Cities Times in December 1956.

In the past 57 years, the Twin Cities have come a long way, but in this Christmas season of 1956 there is, on Johnston Street, on Argyle Street, and on every side street and by-way of our towns, the same spirit of good cheer and friendliness that the pioneers knew. It's a Merry Christmas in the Albernis as it was in 1899.
On the last Christmas Eve in the nineteenth century, coal oil lamps burned late in Bishop's Bakery and in Thomson's General Store next door. Thomson's and the Alberni Trading Store were cleared of their stock of luxury goods-horehounds, peppermints and oranges.
Every chandelier was alight in Armour's Hotel on Argyle Street and the miners were in town from the hills. Glowing and busy were the Arlington bar room and the Alberni Hotel. Prospectors and miners were in town for the holidays and George Drinkwater's Barber Shop (Baths 25 cents)) did a rushing business. The door of Redford's Butcher Shop, Victoria Quay, had been closed after the last roast and chop had been cut from the fresh-killed carcasses of beef and pork.
A group of men gathered that night at Fitzgerald and Burke's livery barn where the horses were given an extra measure of oats and bedded down. Children pulled their stocking caps over their ears as they ran home through the snow. Wood boxes were filled in double quick time and candles were lit on Christmas trees in the towns' few little homes, then boys and girls went to bed to dream of rag dolls, home-made sleds, bows and arrows.

In anticipation of the big dance of the season, Huff's Hall had been swept and decorated. Mrs. Erickson distributed the Christmas mail at her Post Office-home on Victoria Quay and the people of the little towns stopped to talk over news from back East and from the Old Country.
Fifty-six years have passed. Nearly every lot in the downtown areas has its building. Automobiles have taken over from the faithful horses and the taxi stand supercedes the livery stable. Neon signs and electric lights illumine the streets where the old timers carried coal oil lanterns. Merchandise of the Albernis' shops this year is a far cry from the bolts of red flannel, candles, coal oil, castile soap, flour, bacon and beans of 1899, but the greetings exchanged by merchants and customers are as hearty and sincere.

POST OFFICE MYSTERY SOLVED...AND MORE!

It's been gone for over forty-five years, but a lot of people can still remember the grand old Port Alberni Post Office, that stood at the corner of Third and Angus, for almost 50 years.

"It should never have been torn down," some residents still insist today. Others claim it was damaged in the 1946 earthquake and would have cost too much to repair. I did a lot of archival research in 2005 on the City landmark that dominated the downtown area until 1961, when it was demolished in the name of progress. But one question had remained unsolved – What was in the metal box that was enclosed in a cornerstone of the majestic old structure, back in 1914.

Now we know, thanks to some detective work by the local Archives team, who discovered a list of items picked up at the Port Alberni City Hall on March 22, 1967. Apparently the Alberni Valley Historical and Museum Society took possession of a good number of photographs and papers that day – including the contents of the box from the corner stone at the old Post Office, which were:
1. A copy of the Port Alberni News dated June 10, 1914.
2. Picture of the Western Post, end of Canadian Highway, with W.W. Foster Deputy Minister of Works, taken on May 4, 1912.
3. Pictures of Gilbert's Mill, the cottage where Mr. & Mrs. P. Stone of Stone Bros. lived and swimming lake in the present sight of the Assembly Dock.
4. Pictures of the view of Port Alberni from the waterfront – with photos of Buildings; C.P.R. freight shed, cottage of W.R. Ellis, Overwaitea Store, Bird Block, Alberni hardware (C.A. McNaughton), Somass Hotel, Log Boom, G.H. Bird Mill all taken in approximately 1913. This list of the items placed in the metal box was meant to be a type of time capsule almost 100 years ago. It's not known now - just how long residents then - thought the unique-looking structure would last, but it is clear today that the stately building still holds a lot of fond memories for many.

WAIT ! There's more! Read on:

P.S. The March 30th, 1961 issue of the West Coast Advocate carried this story:

"The old Post Office block has been sold to eastern interests according to an unconfirmed report this week.

Following its closure the property was acquired by a syndicate of local persons, who purchased it for speculation purposes. During the past year they have been accepting proposals for purchase of the property. The building will be torn down to permit the expansion of a dept. store."

THEN.... The April 27th, 1961 edition of the West Coast Advocate had this advertisement:

"Old Post Office to be demolished! Auction Sale to be held on Saturday, April 29th at 10am!"

Abe Flanagan was the auctioneer and among the items to go on the block were 5 toilets, 25 doors, 140 windows, and 1 oak counter.

THIS brings me to an interesting footnote on the demolition of the Post Office. While in the Archives recently, I met Jackie Busby (who had written to me almost a year ago about Freethy's Store), and she informed me that the Post office flag pole is in her front yard.

"My late husband, "Rusty" Busby, bought the flag pole at the demolition sale before we were married in 1963," Jackie commented.

"He put it up after we moved to McKenzie Road. It's under 15 feet high."

P. S. The old Post Office Bell that was made in 1915, by a foundry in England, still exists today, although it's in rough shape. Stay tuned, so-to-speak, for more on "the bell."

The bell as it is today.

Photo Courtesy of The Alberni Valley Museum

1955 – WHEN THE ALBERNI VALLEY WAS THE BASKETBALL CAPITOL OF CANADA!

The Alberni Athletics got by the Victoria Orphans to win the Island title, then they downed the Vancouver Clover Leafs to take the Provincials and following a victory over the Edmonton Town Hallers in the Western Canada round, Alberni beat the Sault St. Marie Gunners to take the Canadian Basketball Championship. What a year 1955 was!

Over the next few months I'll be featuring memorable snap shots from some of those games in the old Athletic Hall, courtesy of Gerry Fitzgerald who discovered a fist full of 51 year-old black & white glossy "pics."

Denny Grisdale, a 6 foot, 2-inch Forward for the Athletics in '55, is providing the names of his team mates in each picture.

Number eight in the series: This week a flashback to the court action in the Canadian Senior A Men's Basketball Championship finals between the Athletics and the Sault St. Marie Gunners. All three games were played at the old Athletic Hall. Not only do you see the two "22's" going for the ball in a tense moment, in one of those games, but the picture below clearly shows the famous balcony in the background.

By the way, Alberni's number 22 was Ron Bissett and the "Soo's" number 22 was worn by Lou Lukena. The players on the left, with their backs to the camera are identified as (right to left) #24 for Sault St. Marie, Jerry Kahle, 6 foot 4-inch Centre, #15 for the "A's ,", Doug Brinham, 6 foot, 2-inch Forward, and #21 for the Gunners, Bob Forster, 6 foot, 1 inch Guard. You can also see the Athletics playing coach, #11, Elmer Speidel in the background and on the extreme right you can make out most of the Soo's #31, Damon Godfrey, 5 foot, 9-inch Guard. Before the first game on Thursday, April 14th, which the Athletics won 84-66, MacMillan and Bloedel announced they were donating and installing an illuminated scoreboard and clock, that was formerly in the U.B.C gym. Electricians from Bailey Electric left on Tuesday (April 12th) to remove the clock and auxiliary equipment and re-installing it in the Athletic Hall.

One final note for now, George "Porky" Andrews, former Alberni star and the man who first put the Athletics on the sports map, opened the series by tossing up the first ball. An article in the West Coast Advocate on the day of the first game, had this to say: "Andrews, whose contributions to local and Canadian basketball make him an obvious choice for the duty, is slated to speak in the opening ceremony."

The reporter who wrote the article in question added this:

"After the full limit series up to this point, however, very few people are predicting a three game sweep."

HOW WRONG THEY WERE!

LOOK AT THE 1957 MEMORY THAT "FLEW IN"

Jim Rutherford Jr. sent his dad in with this 1957 picture taken at Air Cadet Summer Camp in Abbotsford. Yes, teenage Jim is in the photo (second from the left in the back row, see the circle), but look at the names below to see how many other local boys were in the "609 Squadron" almost 50 years ago.

Back Row, left to right: Jim Cates, Jim Rutherford Jr., Gerald Peters, Eric Oscarson, Unknown, Jack Ellis, Bill Windley, Albert Dore, Harry Dyler, Jack Tyler and Frank Merx. Middle Row, left to right: Unknown, Unknown, Gil Dore, Unknown, Unknown, Ray Nicklin, Unknown, Bill Davenock and __Didier. Front Row, left to right: Unknown, Ritchie Startup, Bob Moore, Terry Power, Bill Ohs, Keith Rumney and John Moen.

Clutesi Haven Marina named on Feb. 14, 1973

A group of anonymous judges selected a high school student's suggestion as the winning entry in the "Marina Naming Contest", sponsored by the Port Alberni Port Authority 37 years ago.

Theresa Kingston won the $50 prize for submitting "Clutesi's Haven". In support of her entry, Miss Kingston wrote:

"This was once all Indian land and George Clutesi has done a lot for his people in keeping alive their culture and love of nature."

A few days later, on Feb. 19, Meg Trebett had this to say in her column in the Alberni Valley Times:

"I like the judges' choice. I'm glad that George Clutesi's work and talents are being given recognition in the name. The judges' comment when they announced that Theresa Kingston's submission Clutesi's Haven had been chosen was "many entries used the Clutesi name but haven was chosen as the best describing a port or harbour."

The only thing that bothers me is that Clutesi is bound to be mispronounced. It irritates me to hear the word pronounced Clu-tessi, with the emphasis on the second syllable. But then some people say Kisutskis when they mean Kitsuksis, Sumass for Somass and Sprout for Sproat."

It turns out that Meg's concern about people mispronouncing Clutesi was well founded – it still happens almost 4 decades later, and many people (most longtime residents who live out there) still say Sprout Lake.

I also felt what was interesting in Meg Trebett's observations back in 1973, was some of the 371 names suggested, like "Knot's Tie-Up", "Alberni Anchors" or "The Happy Boaters Marina".

Meg also pointed out that some folks suggested naming the new Marina after local pioneers like Capt. Huff, the man who built a wharf on the Somass near Kitsuksis Creek in 1892. Others wanted it named after well-known residents like Fred Bishop, Reece Riley, Denny O'Brien or John Grieve. A dozen or more referred to the 1964 Tidal Wave, while many of the names contained the word Tyee and made reference to fishing in the Alberni Inlet.

"We liked the one suggesting Somass Marina because it's near the river and the drug store," Meg wrote.

As history has recorded, the 200-berth Clutesi Haven Marina was officially opened on June 29, 1973. Approximately 150 officials and guests, including Theresa Kingston and George Clutesi, were in attendance when former Port Alberni Harbour Commission chairman Dennis O'Brien and Ald. Howard McLean cut the ribbon.

School Started in 1914 for Cherry Creek!

Photo courtesy of the Provincial archives.

Cherry Creek School, a one-room building, opened in 1914. This picture was taken a few years later, according to the information I've gathered. A brand new, larger school was built on the same site (at Cherry Creek Road and Cowley) in 1950. It served the area well for over half a century (with some modifications) until "declining enrollment" and budget deficits forced it's closure in 2003, along with four other schools.(those were Beaver Creek Elementary, Sproat Elementary, Redford Elementary and Mt. Klitsa Jr. Secondary)

More on Toms Bros. Ltd.....

A few weeks ago I wrote about Toms Bros. Ltd. in 1956, when the business was on Fourth Avenue. Harold Doucette reminded me that Ken and Art Toms actually purchased an existing small trucking business in 1945 and changed the name. The brothers bought out George Shead, who had started a transfer, and taxi business in 1914, on Third Avenue. The office, stables and garage were right where Merit Furniture is today. In 1947, Ken & Art Toms built the modern premises (which you saw in the photo I ran a few weeks ago) on Fourth Avenue, where they had the facilities to service their own fleet of trucks, as well as the general public's vehicles. TOMS BROS. had up to 20 trucks and drivers on the road during peak times transporting lumber from the local mills, long distance hauling, moving and storage, plus a large sawdust fuel business. In 1962, Woodwards Dept. Store wanted to expand (see photo on page 2) so Ken & Art sold their property, and moved to Roger Street, where they built a large storage facility. Then, in May, 1970, the brothers caught the retirement bug selling out to Harold Doucette, who still operates TOMS BROS. LTD, today, with his family, on Glenwood a short distance from the Roger Street location. What a great example of a local business that's over 90 years old and still going strong. George Shead would be very happy today.

A "Lotta Logs"...

The year was 1948! George Dingsdale stopped on Margaret Street (between Southgate & Johnston, across from the Arlie I'm told) for a "photo-op" with his large load of logs. The information given to me years ago was that this haul scaled out to 6,249 feet, and that drivers like George made twenty dollars per trip almost 60 years ago. I am in the process of confirming this, and if you have anything to offer, or have "logging stories and photos" of your own, please call me or drop any items off at the Pennyworth office on Margaret Street.

This picture showing George Shead and his "trusty taxi" on Third Avenue, appeared in the November 1964 issue of the "Western Wonderland," a monthly magazine that served the interest of the Pacific Northwest.

Remember Port Alberni's Fire Hall..at 5th & Argyle??

Before amalgamation of the Twin Cities in 1967, and the move of both volunteer fire departments to a modern facility at Tenth & Bute, Port Alberni's Fire Hall for many years was located behind the police station at Fifth and Argyle. Rob Mah captured the scene first in 1949, then again in the late '60's.(after the new building was opened)

Hi Ike,
I took quite a few pictures of buildings around town. Losing the old Port Alberni Post Office was a sad event. The old Port Alberni Fire Hall stood prominently for many years behind the old Police Station on Argyle. The picture on the left was taken during the May 24th, 1949 parade, as it passes by the Police Station, with the Fire Hall in the background. That's Alex Taylor, Mayor of Teen Town in the car as it turns to go down to Recreation Park(the building which would become the paramount theatre, had not been constructed to the extreme right) The photo on the right shows the vacant building almost 20 years later.(note* the empty lot on the right indicates the police station was already demolished and you can see part of the paramount theatre on the extreme right) Thanks Ike, more to come.
Rob

What do you know about this picture?

This is the first in a series of pictures that Jim Robertson found recently in some old files at Coast Realty.
"This building was at the corner of Gertrude and Southgate," Jim offered. "I don't know when it was taken though."
I know that Kennedy Motors was at this location in the late fifties, and later Somass Tire occupied the corner. Of course, the Southgate Centre came after that. What does this picture say to you? Lets share the history at: ikepatterson@telus.net or leave a message for me at 250-723-8171.
Watch for more of Jim's "file photos" in the coming weeks and remember, whenever you come across any interesting pictures of our past, please contact me.

January 20, 1913

A picture of the first elected council of the city of Alberni taken on January 20, 1913, the date of the first meeting.

(left to right) John Grieve, Frank Gibson, Alan W. Neill, C. Frederic Bishop (mayor), George Forrest, James Hills, George A. Spencer

AILI JOWSEY... A FASCINATING, SCRUPULOUSLY HONEST AND KINDLY PERSON

Jennifer believes this snapshot of Jack and Aili was taken in Vancouver by one of those souvenir street photographers in 1937.

Mother and Daughters get together at Fir Park Village in October of 2003 left to right Doris, Mavis and Frances with their Mom.

Ike's Note: I had many discussions with Aili and Jack Jowsey over the many years I was with CJAV and they both worked in the store. Aili always impressed me as the type of person who didn't' just talk about doing things, she did them. Jowsey's customers used to praise her "helping them over the hard times" with extended credit, sometimes even a small loan. Heaven knows I conversed with thousands of people just in those first ten years of living "on the air" and whenever Aili's name was mentioned, then or in later years, in conjunction with Jowsey's or any other issue folks always spoke with the highest respect. Now with permission and assistance from Aili's granddaughter Jennifer Norn, let's pay tribute to AILI JOWSEY...

Aili Jowsey life story reads like a novel, that would be a best seller and certainly be made into a great movie. She was born Aili Agnes Markkula in Mac-Crorie, Saskatchewan, the daughter of Victor and Wilhelmina Markkula, poor immigrants from rural Finland. Aili grew up with her parents and her brother victor among many other Finnish immigrants in Saskatchewan, learning English as soon as she started school. She met her future husband Jack Jowsey at school and they would go to dances at the local Finn hall. They were married in 1934, and had two daughters, Doris and Mavis Jowsey.

Jack wasn't keen on farming so he and Aili moved to Alberni in 1937, where jack worked at the mill and at Carter's Hardware store on Johnston (later to become Bronson's)

Then in 1947, he and Aili started "Jowsey's Home Variety and Electric" on Johnston where the store is still located today. Aili worked at Jowsey's, with her mother moving to Alberni to take care of the children, including Jennifer's mother, Frances who was born a year after the store opened.

Besides working Aili found the time to be a Girl Guide leader, a Soroptimist Club Member and always a committed CCF (later NDP) member. Gerard Janssen recalled at Aili's memorial service "both Dave Barrett and Tommy Douglas used to stop in at Jowsey's to chat with Aili and Jack about Alberni politics."

Retirement to Qualicum came next for Aili and Jack leaving their daughter Frances and son-in law Brian Dodsworth (Jennifer's parents) to run the store. I can remember quite a few times after retirement, seeing them come over for a visit to Jowsey's, obviously proud of the job being done, but always ready with helpful advice.

In 1982, after being happily married for 47 years, Aili's Life took an unexpected turn, when Jack passed away. Although deeply saddened, Aili was determined to remain engaged in life, so she joined the "Happy Wanderers", travelling all over the world, including yearly trips to Hawaii. She joined Elder College, studied poetry, literature, current events and history.

When Frances was confided to a wheelchair by arthritis, Aili was there to tend to the family. She was a "phoner" for the NDP party and eventually a resident of Fir Park Village until she passed away on March 31st at the age of 91. Aili Jowsey, a truly wonderful person who is sorely missed by many. I am proud to say I knew her.

Photos courtesy of Jennifer Norn

Memories of Jowsey's

To celebrate the 63rd anniversary of Jowsey's Furniture & Appliances, Jennifer and Mark Norn held a "memory" contest. Customers, and former customers, were invited to write down their favourite memory of the legendary business started by Jennifer's grandparents, Jack and Aili Jowsey, back in 1947.

"Margaret Bowen's memory won," Jennifer announced recently. "She won a Simmons queen size mattress and box spring. We would also like to award a $100 gift card to another entry, but it was not signed. If the author of the "mystery memory" would please contact the store, we would appreciate it very much."

Now, the mystery entry, titled "Jowsey's memories"

"My first memory of Jowsey's store goes back to the days when it was a variety store. I was newly married and we bought our first Xmas decorations from Mrs. Jowsey (wax snowmen), they decorated my mantel for at least the next 25 years.

The variety store began to change. Gone was the paint department; in came appliances, TV's and so on. Jowsey's always changed with the times. In the store, the faces of Mr. and Mrs. Jowsey, Harry and Mildred greeted you. As time went on, Brian, Fran, Doug and of course Mildred, she was there forever.

The one memory that stands out is the "clothes dryer". We built our home in the mid fifties and always planned on having an automatic washing machine but never a clothes dryer. Jack Jowsey had the nerve to tell us that one day every home would have a dryer. I thought, "give up my clothes line and rack; nerve."

Well, he was right! Then he told us most homes would have a dishwasher – I did think the poor man had lost it. But time would tell and he was right. Jack was a visionary, always looking ahead, adding this, taking away that, always making the store better. I am sure the day Jennifer was born he looked at her and said one day you will run the store. Once again, he was right!

Over the many years, the faces may have changed, but the welcome mat has always been the same. It is always a pleasure to drop in the store just to say hi, pass the time of day and sometimes make a purchase."

Jennifer also discovered some slides, believed to be from the late 60's, and had them developed as photos.

"Among those slides were two about the business," she explained. "One is my dad, Brian Dodsworth, knitting in the Jowsey's booth at the Fall Fair, and the other shows Aili and Jack admiring a new van in the store's parking lot."

MORE ON THE ARGYLE ATHLETIC CLUB STORY

With Jim Spencer's input we've established the approximate date (1934) that the photo was taken and the location on Argyle Street.

NOW... jump ahead about ten years to Sunday, October 1st, 1944, when fire destroyed the Port Alberni Hotel and Café, along with MacGregors Men's Wear Store (both were in the same building).

As you can see, this picture taken by Gordon Jackson at the time, shows the north side of Argyle from the famous "cottage" building at First & Argyle down to the Somass Hotel.

The arrows indicate where the girls were standing in 1934 and where the Argyle Athletic Club was located in the basement of the old hotel.

After an interview last September with former Port Alberni resident Floyd "Abe" Abrahamson, I went back to research this story some more. Thanks to Floyd's great memory, I discovered the correct date of the fire was October 1st, 1944, not October 30th, 1942 originally given to me last April. Floyd recalled the buildings were still there when he came to the Valley in January, 1943, as a Provincial Police Officer. Lo and behold, he was right!

TO ADD FURTHER PERSPECTIVE... less than two years later, on May 6, 1946, Woodward's relocated to Port Alberni, taking over the Waterhouse and Greene premises on the bottom floor of the Somass Hotel. Then less than a year after that, on February 17, 1947, fire would strike the Somass Hotel, destroying the rear portion of the legendary building.. Why is that important to our original story about the old Port Alberni Hotel? Well, the photos that recorded the unreal response to Woodward's "fire sale" show a big hole on Argyle, confirming where the Port Alberni Hotel building, with the Argyle Athletic Club was, when that picture from last week's column was taken. Talk about connections!

THIS SUNDAY IS MARTIN MARS WATER BOMBER DAY!

The Coulson Group of Companies invites the entire Community to share in the opening day celebrations of their new " Martin Mars Fire Base" at Sproat Lake this Sunday, July 8th, from noon to 4pm.

The opening ceremony at 2:30pm will also feature a famous "water drop". Enjoy free hot dogs and cake, browse through the new Gift shop that's loaded with souvenirs and take a tour of this active fire fighting facility that's never been open to the public before.

"We've created a display area next to the gift shop," Darlene Coulson pointed out. "Besides the life history of the Mars, people will get a good look at various parts, including one of the Bomber's 18 cylinder – 3350 cubic inch – engines."

This is one of the most sought after "Mars photos" and my personal favourite. This "dramatic picture" was taken on June 20, 1973, during the Hunter's Store blaze on Highway 4 and it was the first time the Martin Mars was ever used to put out a residential fire. It was indeed one of the most memorable moments for everyone there, including me.
Thanks to Pete Aspinall at the Port Alberni Fire Dept. for providing this "great moment in time."

Sunday's "Open House" is really a "Community Day" because the Coulson family would like to thank everyone for the response received when it was announced that the Mars Bombers would be staying here. "We were so amazed by the out pouring of emotion," Darlene revealed. "People sent us flowers, people came up to myself, Wayne, all of our family, in tears. It just gives me goose bumps even to talk about it because there was so much emotion and there's so much pride in ownership of these wonderful planes."

You have seen many times in "This Was Then" how "ironic" it is that past events always seem to be "connected" Well Darlene has found that's true with the Mars and the Coulson family.
"It's so interesting, I find the Mars first landed here in 1960 which is the year Coulson Forest Products began. Wayne and I just think that's a great connection - that the Mars have been flying for 47 years and that's how long our Company has been in business."

Plans are to have the Martin Mars Fire Base open 7 days a week, from 11am to 4pm, following this Sunday's "Opening Day Celebrations." Three "tour guides" will be on hand to answer questions and to tell stories about these "legendary" Water Bombers, which happen to be the only two Martin Mars aircraft left in the world.
For more information go to the new website www.martinmars.com or click on to www.coulsongroup.com and take the link to Coulson Flying Tankers.

**The Martin Mars Fire Base is located on Bomber Base Road, just off Highway 4, at Sproat Lake Park (watch for the signs).
PLEASE NOTE****
 Because of limited parking at the base itself, a shuttle bus will run from the Sproat Lake Park "boat launch parking lot," from 11:45am to 4pm this Sunday.

LOOK WHAT JAN JANSMA FOUND – in a 1949 Magazine!
A 58 year-old article that has special meaning for the Alberni Valley.

hobby HALL OF FAME

Mr. Martin takes a craftsman's pride in his models as he contrasts his giant Mars to his frail pioneer "motor kite."

GLENN L. MARTIN – AIR CRAFTSMAN

NEVER can tell how a lad will turn out. Now look at Glenn L. (for Luther) Martin, biggest plane builder in America. At three years of age he dismantled a cultivator all by himself—or so the family story claims. But then, instead of sticking to farm problems and figuring out better ways to till the good earth, he went and flew a kite—and decided to make aviation his career.

One of the first kites he built was a tailless box that soared almost vertically and stood the kids on their heads with envy. Young Glenn turned his living room into a factory and produced three a day at 25 cents each—payable on the installment plan.

The first of the long line of Martin planes was a motorized version of this toy. In 1909 he took it aloft, becoming the third man in the U. S. to fly a self-made plane.

A master craftsman of the air, Mr. Martin makes a lot finer and faster "motor kites" now—such as the 200-foot seaplane Mars, the six-jet bomber XB-48 and Gorgon IV, a new pilotless ramjet aircraft. But he gets his greatest thrill out of showing visitors some of the 100 model planes he's made himself or collected—especially his favorite handiwork, the miniature of the big box kite that first flew him into his fabulous career as aviation's No. 1 air craftsman. •

Mrs. Minta Martin, at 85, is still keen on her son's collection. She helped build—and fly—his first plane.

Mechanix Illustrated

Who could have predicted that a 1949 story about Glenn L. Martin, the man affectionately known as 'the father of the Martin Mars', would one day have a direct connection to us in the Alberni Valley.

Even after the 'Caroline Mars', the first 'flying boat'- to be converted into a water bomber – arrived at Sproat Lake in September of 1959, no one could have guessed the impact that Mr. Martin's creations would have here in the following decades.

As history has recorded, the Caroline Mars was one of the fleet of four purchased to fight forest fires in BC by the then "Forest Industries Flying Tankers' (FIFT) of which M & B was a major player. The Caroline Mars had not been converted when it first arrived at Sproat Lake and was used as a training tool for the ground and flight crews until late autumn.

The 'Marianas Mars' was the first to be converted to its water bomber role by Fairley Aviation of Victoria and took up duty at Sproat Lake in the spring of 1960. It was a short lived tour though, because on June 23, 1960, the Marianas crashed, killing all four crew members. The tragic accident was chalked up to a bad decision by a less experienced captain.

The Caroline's conversion was put on fast forward and she proved that the world's largest sea planes could effectively extinguish forest fires when she took on a pair of blazes within three days in 1962. The Mars and FIFT were hailed as 'overnight sensations'.

The fame was put on 'pause' however, when the Caroline Mars, which was at Pat Bay that winter and was destroyed by Hurricane Freida. The remaining two Mars aircraft, the 'Philippine and Hawaii', were converted and arrived on station when the 1963 fire season started.

Over 40 years later, the last two Martin Mars are still operating out of their Sproat Lake base, but under the private ownership of 'The Coulson Group of Companies', started by the Coulson family in 1960, when the Caroline Mars first landed here.

30th Annual Terry Fox Run goes Sunday, September 19

It was September 2, 1981 when Doug Brimacombe, (left), then Parks & Recreation superintendent, was spreading the news about the first Terry Fox Run by presenting t-shirts to Mayor Jim Robertson, Al Robinson, director of instruction for School District 70 and Bernard Kimble, MB's manger of community relations.
This year, the 30th Annual Terry Fox Run will be held at the Somass Legion Branch 169 on Sunday, September 19.

As the AV Lions Club prepares for this year's Terry Fox Run, the 30th annual affair, it's a good time to look back to September 1981 when Port Alberni joined dozens of other communities across the country for the first Terry Fox "Marathon of Hope" run.

One hundred and eighty-six Valley residents ran, walked and roller-skated on Sept. 13, 1981, raising over $1800. They were among the millions of Canadians who collected an anticipated additional $5 million to combat the cancer that took Fox's life that June.

"The turnout was pretty good," Garry Korven, sports program coordinator at Echo Centre remarked. "The oldest participant was 76, and the youngest six, according to the entry forms. First to finish was 21 year old Cody Redford with a time of 38 minutes and 20 seconds."

1981's event was co-sponsored by Parks & Recreation and the Valley Roadrunners Club. The start and finish was at A.W. Neil School.

The 2010 30th Annual Terry Fox Run on Sunday, Sept. 19 will be headquartered at the Somass Legion on Victoria Quay, and is once again sponsored by the Lions Club.

"Registration starts at 9 a.m., with the run starting at 10:00 precisely," event organizer Robert Dalton emphasized. "We'll be doing the Kitsuksis Dyke and folks have a choice of going 2, 5 or 10 kilometres."

Robert will be presenting "30 year participation certificates" to honour those participants who have supported the Terry Fox Run throughout the past 30 years.

About the Glen L. Martin story.

Jan Jansma, a regular 'This Was Then' reader and contributor, found it in the February 1949 issue of 'Mechanix Illustrated', a magazine he has had for over 50 years.

"I got it back in the mid '50's when I first got to Canada," Jan recalled. "I spent a bit of time working in Taber, Alberta, before coming to Port Alberni on February 7th, 1956."

Remembering the Two Spot

This picture showing some of the 35 volunteers at work on the Two Spot was taken at the city works yard in the last week of May, 1983. The five crews of workers had the loan of equipment and Alberni Engineering when restoring the 42 ton Shay logging locomotive.

THIS SUNDAY MARKS 25 YEARS FOR LOGGERS SPORTS – AT THE FALL FAIR!

But old timers can remember the events from over 60 years ago.

"There are pictures in my family album of us, when I was a very small boy, at Recreation Park watching Loggers Sports back in the 1940's," Al Boyko told me during the recent raising of the two new climbing poles at the Fair grounds. "Those pictures were taken near the end of the Second World War. I can remember, as a young lad, when they climbed the trees that were in the back of the Park. They never even took the top off, they just limbed off a bunch of branches and up they went."

After Recreation Park, the Elks Lodge ran Loggers Sports out at Sproat Lake Park on the 24th of May weekend for a number of years.

"They put on a very small mediocre program with $300 in prize money for the whole day," Al remarked.

"I remember being a spectator there in 1962 watching the loggers that came in thinking by golly it wouldn't be hard to beat these guys and it wasn't."

Al reckons Loggers Sports started in 1961 or '62 out at the Lake and lasted until 1970.

"In 1971 it was moved to Shoemaker Bay Road in what was called the Timber Bowl," Al explained. "There was a group of us that got together and received property and funding from a very generous company, MacMillan Bloedel. When we took it over, we raised the prize money to $3,000."

Then in 1983, a home was created for Loggers Sports at the Fall Fair grounds.

"For many years the ad hoc group that I was associated with, called the Port Alberni Loggers Sports Committee (a mixture of people who volunteered their time) kept the tradition alive here in the community," Al remarked. "Now, there is a handful of members left from that group and we're on the threshold of our 25th anniversary here with the Fall Fair. We are members of the Canadian Loggers Sports Association for the simple fact that we want to have the correct rules, get the mailings and the championships."

Did Al Boyko ever think Loggers Sports would have lasted this long?

"Well, it has got longevity, as long as there are loggers working out in the woods because loggers are proud people," Al observed. "Based on the fact that they have to go out there and face the elements and the hazards that are associated with every facet of the forest industry, it doesn't matter what it is, and people who work in that industry are

very proud of the fact that they survived it and work at it."

Even if the day comes when there is no more logging in the bush, many folks believe Loggers Sports would still be a crowd-pleaser.

"It could be," Al offered. "I've gone to a lot of other communities and a lot of other cities that have never seen a log and the stands are always full when they see the loggers come in."

Be in the stands at the Fair Grounds this Sunday when Al Boyko will be back behind the microphone describing the action of yet another exciting Loggers Sports Show. Registration starts at 9am, with the preliminaries at 10:00 and the opening ceremonies start at noon. Remember your admission to the Fall Fair gets you a free seat at the Timber Bowl.

This picture, courtesy of Butch Marocchi, shows the previous climbing poles being delivered and installed at the Fair Grounds in May, 1993. Island Timberlands donated the two new poles that are in place for this year's show on Sunday.

These photos were taken during one of the years that Loggers Sports was held at Sproat Lake Park. They were given to me some time ago, but when they were taken (between 1962-1970) and who is in them remains unknown. Feel free to pass along any details at: ikepatterson@telus.net or call me at 250-723-3709.

P. Y. Marine on 4th Avenue since 1981

Paul and Elizabeth Yuen, standing on the left, at the grand opening of their new facility on Fourth Avenue on Saturday, March 7, 1981. Cutting the ribbon is OMC District Manager, Jim Carslake, and the man responsible for construction of the building, Cecil Peffers, is on the far right.

Paul Yuen and outboard motors go back to 1958. Many local boaters can probably recall when Paul was part of the Woodward's Marine team and when he started P.Y. Marine at Third & Napier back in March 1979, but many others will undoubtedly remember when Paul and Elizabeth relocated to their brand new location at 3680 4th Avenue 29 years ago.

"We moved on Boxing Day, 1980," Elizabeth remarked. "We were open and running on January 2, 1981."

This year, Paul and Elizabeth are not only marking 29 years on 4th Avenue, but also celebrating the 31st anniversary of P.Y. Marine.

"Service is still our main concern, just like it was when we started," Paul emphasized. "We want to quietly let everyone know that we're still here and to thank our many customers for their continued support over the years."

Make a note to take a few minutes next Wednesday, March 24, for a stop by P.Y. Marine to reminisce over free coffee and doughnuts.

Feel free to bring in those outboard motor stories too.

The Loonie arrived in 1987

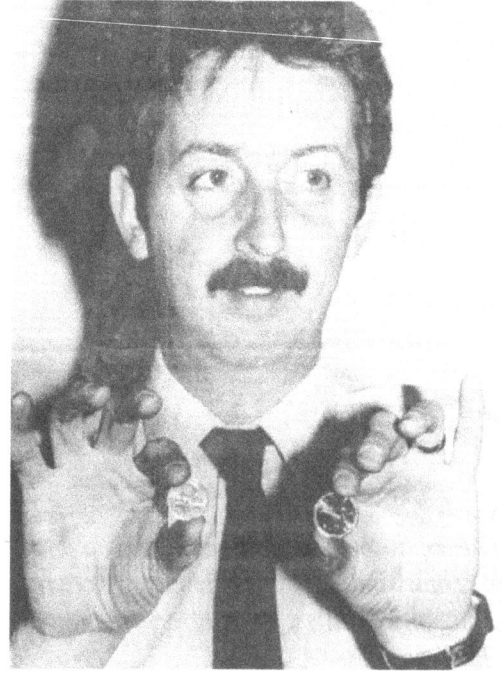

John Richardson, AV Times circulation manager 23 years ago, showed everyone the money (the new loonie, that is) in this picture that appeared in the paper on July 6, 1987. Yes, some of the local banks already had some of the 35 million loonies, which had been distributed nationally on June 30. The 11-sided coins, featuring a loon on one side and Queen Elizabeth on the other, were scheduled to replace the one-dollar bill by the end of 1989.

Today, the loonie is everywhere of course, the one-dollar bill is a collector's item (like the penny will be soon), but John Richardson is still the circulation manager at the Times.

What did you think about the introduction of a one-dollar coin back then? Did you save one of the first loonies you received in change?

August 1990 – Matthew Kittle meets Wayne Gretzky

Local hockey player Matthew Kittle (left) along with Jordy Behan of Powell River, met hockey's "Great One" in Toronto August 13-14, 1990. They were among more than 50 children between the ages of 7 and 15 who took part in a hockey camp in which instruction was provided by Wayne Gretzkey, his father Walter, Luc Robitaille, Kirk Muller and Ed Olczyk. The participants were randomly selected following local competitions earlier in the year.

A CONVERSATION WITH ART WYNANS
Legendary businessmen going strong after 50 years

One warm afternoon recently, I went to probably the most relaxing place in town-upstairs at Wynan's Furniture on Merrifield. Surrounded by 15,000 square feet of quality home furnishings, I listened as a group of long-time customers visited with Art. "I love coming here" One lady exclaimed. "It's like walking into my house, heck it should, everything I have, I got from Art." When you remember Wynans has been open in various locations on both sides of town for over fifty years, this scenario is not unusual.

It all started for Art, in Port Alberni on November 17, 1955, when he opened his first store on Argyle Street. I had heard his story before, back in the late '60's in the new store he had built at Second &Angus. It's a tale of hard work in the upholstery and custom made furniture business –a business Art learned from his father, uncle and grandfather in Holland, before coming to Canada in October 1952. After about three and a half years working in a Nanaimo upholstery shop, Art brought his skills to the Alberni Valley and over fifty years later he is still practicing his trade here.

"Upholstery, draperies and furniture repairs are still the biggest part of our business," Art told me. "Our good past has given us good customer relationships today."

Speaking of the furniture business today, Art reflects on the fact that people used to take more time shopping, with the idea of selecting items they would keep for a long time, often placing custom orders on in store display merchandise.

"Folks today are in a big hurry and there are more discount stores competing for their business," said Art. "But you still get what you pay for."

Away from furniture for a moment. As we reminisced about the valley over the past five decades, I was reminded that Art can speak with authority on other subjects such as cycling, local politics and barbequing salmon for thousands of people in a single weekend. Art is easy to talk with, so when adding to your home's wardrobe, pay a relaxing visit to Wynans, Where "furniture is still Art."

REMEMBERING A "LAND MARK BUSINESS"...
This picture of Tyler's Jewellers, on Gertrude, is believed to have been taken after 1952 and prior to 1955, by the late Bob Gray.

Courtesy of AV Museum #PN15936 - From the Bob Gray "City Works Dept." Collection

When I first saw the Tyler's Jewellers picture above, I remembered that building from an earlier photo (see insert). It was an ad for 'Lloyd & Walker Jewellers' on Gertrude Street in the September 11th, 1947 issue of Island Events and I had put it in the 2nd Volume of 'The Best of This Was Then" in May of 2006.

After that supplement went out, Doris McKenzie, of Port McNeill, emailed to say:
"Our dad and mom, Ray and Evaline Tyler, bought out Mr. Lloyd in the early '50's and then bought out Mr. Walker (we're not positive but we think) around 1952 and it became Tyler's Jewellers. The store was located in what is now Jowsey's parking lot. Dad and mom moved the jewellery store to Argyle Street around 1960."

Since I now have more information in my possession, I was able to follow up on that 2006 item and response. The 1951 and '52 local phone books showed "Tyler & Walker Watchmakers & Jewellers," Ray Tyler – Brian Walker, on Gertrude Street. Those same phone books also show "Lloyd's Credit Jewellers" at 116 First Avenue North (across from the Good Eats Café). Also, as early as March, 1948, ads for "Lloyd's Jewellers – Clothiers" at 116 1st avenue, started showing up in issues of "Island Events." Unless there were two Lloyds at the time, it would appear that Mr. Lloyd opened his own store in Port Alberni as early as 1948, after selling to the Tylers in Alberni.

The 1955 phone book shows only "Tyler's Jewellers" at 320 Gertrude, so that would indicate Walker was bought out sometime after March 1952 and no later that the end of 1954. In 1957's phone book, the listing for Tyler's Jewellers still showed 320 Gertrude, but it also showed a "George's Jewellery & Gift Shop" at 209 Argyle Street (the location where Tyler's would move to) and those were still the same in 1959. A check in the 1960 "City Directory" reveals that George Chalifour had relocated George's Jewellery to 216 Third Avenue South and Tyler's Jewellers had moved to 209 Argyle.

This would seem to confirm Doris's story about her parents buying into Lloyd & Walker Jewellers, changing it to Tyler's Jewellers and then relocating to Argyle Street. Now, I'll work on when the Tylers sold out to the late Al Dievert who created Dievert's Jewellers, a business that his daughter and son-in-law continue to operate today in the Adelaide Centre, a block and a half away from 320 Gertrude Street where the Tylers started a lifetime ago.

65

Here's the largest fish ever caught in the P.A. Salmon Festival

Visit the Chamber of Commerce office and Info Centre to catch a glimpse of the 60 pound, eight ounce Tyee that won the 1982 Derby, and remains the largest winner ever caught in the Port Alberni Salmon Festival. Art Berlinski nailed the monster 28 years ago and no angler has snagged a bigger one yet. However, there is always this year.

In the picture above (taken Aug. 25, 1983) four locals pose with the legendary "big fish" when it was mounted at the Chamber office, left to right, Bob Cole, president of the Salmon Festival Committee, Rob Duncan, president of the AV Chamber of Commerce, Don Jones, treasurer for the Salmon festival, and Bud Schroeder, first vice-president AVCC.

August 1988 – new gardens unveiled at Rollin Art Centre

Rob Dom, president of the Community Arts Council, puts the finishing touches on the new bandstand in the Rollin Art Centre gardens two days before the official opening on August 20, 1988.

The bandstand was built by Dom and Barry Blair, based on a structure that was at the foot of Argyle Street decades ago. Because of a large donation from the organization, it was called the Kiwanis Bandstand.

In all, the three sections of the new garden, estimated to cost $200,000, were highlighted on that special day 22 years ago.

COMING SOON...THE STORY OF "DANA LODGE"! Did you ever stay at "Cupid's Lodge"?

This is how Dana Lodge looked, shortly after opening in 1946 at 509 North Park Drive (now 4701 North Park Drive). The house is still there today and has been lovingly restored over the last number of years by the last two owners.

I recently had the most fascinating story literally delivered to my office in a dilapidated old trunk, which was made in the early 1900's. A name in that trunk lead me to a close friend of the creators of Dana Lodge, Ejner "Luke" Christiansen and his wife, Ruth. The contents of the about-to-be-tossed-out trunk and the help of the friend have allowed me to pass on a heart warming saga of real Valley history that might have been lost forever.

While I am piecing the details together for future release, I would like to hear from the many "boarders" and "friends" that the "Chris's" (as Ruth and Luke were affectionately called) had over more than 30 years at Dana Lodge.

The 1985 boxing match that never happened

Neon Leon Spinks was supposed to meet Flash Gordon Racette in a heavyweight boxing match in Nanaimo on Friday, October 25, 1985 – But it never happened!

Fight promoters said Spinks backed out of the bout because of a rib injury. The former world champion was attempting a comeback after taking the world crown from Muhammad Ali in 1978 but losing it on a rematch.

"I know he (Racette) is a pretty good fighter..He's pretty tough," Spinks told reporters at a press conference on the Tuesday (Oct. 22) before the fight. "But I'm a little bit better."

Port Alberni-raised Racette, billed as British Columbia's Gord Racette, also announced that he was ready for Spinks.

"I'm expecting a hard opponent," Racette said. "But I'm also expecting to win..I don't expect it to go the distance."

Leon Spinks and Gord Racette "put up their dukes" for the cameras on October 22, 1985, a few days before their scheduled heavyweight boxing match-up in Nanaimo. That turned out to be as close as the two would get, because the fight was called off.

Have you ever seen an historical bracelet like this before?

Bob Graham discovered this rare piece of jewelry recently. I believe this "5 most amazing things about Port Alberni" souvenir bracelet (I think it's silver) dates from the late forties up to the late fifties. What do you think? Bob would like to know the history behind this item, and if anyone else still has one. The panels on the bracelet are, from left to right, the BC Flag, Somass River, Cathedral Grove, Sproat Falls, Tyee, and Stamp River Falls.

More on that historical Port Alberni bracelet

Ev Towle sent these pictures of that special, decades-old bracelet.
"I believe that it is most likely pewter and the joining rings are not silver but a gold/brass colour," she explained. "I still can't remember who gave it to me so the date is still murky. I may have gotten it for myself, in which case would possibly have been from the Nootka House."

Ev (Miller) Towle emailed after seeing the "5 most amazing things about Port Alberni" souvenir bracelet story in the Feb. 17 issue.

"Some time ago I mentioned this piece to you – never got around to following it up," Ev wrote. "It is from the late 50's or early '60's (hopefully my memory will pop the answer out at 3 a.m. and I'll be able to give you the exact date). I still have mine and I believe it is a special piece that was commissioned, but due to the price was not accepted for sale. It may have been a product of the Gyro Club or the Chamber of Commerce. Alternately, it could have been sold out of the Nootka House."

Ev said her bracelet has a broken link, but she would send photos to confirm it's the same as the one Bob Graham brought in.

"By the way, Ike, I have seen mention of the Franklin Camp and others in This Was Then," Ev added. "My father (G.T. Miller) had the contract to paint camps and schools all up and down the coast. If the buildings were turquoise and green, he painted them in the very late 40's or very early 50's. Maybe that would help date some photos."

SIXTY YEARS AGO...

January 22nd – Mr. and Mrs. George Bird celebrate their 58th wedding anniversary. Mr. Bird came to the Valley with his wife in 1892. He was a member of Port Alberni's first City Council in 1912. (Taken from the Vancouver Daily Province)

June 24th – The sum of $16,246.41 had been collected in the Alberni District for the benefit of flood victims of the Fraser valley. Of this amount, $10,655.13 was secured by radio station CJAV. (Taken from the West Coast Advocate)

FIFTY YEARS AGO...

April 5th – A mighty charge of high explosives – man's greatest non-atomic blast – was set off in the heart of "Ripple Rock" near Campbell River. The tremendous explosion, designed to decapitate the West Coast's worst underwater shipping menace, was set off at 9:31am, minutes before the area was deluged by rain. (Taken from The Daily Free Press)

The Johnny Massop story continues
John "T" the Drifter – by his brother Theo

This picture appeared in the Alberni Valley Times (Spectrum section) on Friday, June 1, 1973. The original caption read:
Johnny Massop's old band broke up recently but the Port Alberni musician (third from the left) and his younger brother Ted (left) recruited two new members and formed the J & T Combination, a popular band which is drawing large and appreciative audiences and has just taped two original songs. Drummer Don Bergen, formerly with the Lulu Islanders and Wade Tourangeau, a local bass player, round out the group, which hopes to have a single-playing record on the market in four to six weeks. The record, on Jim Rutherford's Custom Sound label, contains songs composed by the Massop brothers, "Will I Ever See her Again?" by Ted and "I Never Meant to Be Untrue" by Johnny.

I could write a book about the life and times of this man. Here is a small excerpt.

In 1968, as a young musician, embarking upon my adolescence and a performing career, my brother John approached me and said, "So you want to be a performing musician, well let me show you the ropes." That was not the first, or only time, John took me under his wing to show me what I needed to know in this world. In this case he taught me how to hustle for gigs, how to deal with other musicians, how to handle a stage and a lot of stuff that my parents may not have been happy about me learning. All part of what a musician faces in this life.

I suppose some of the greatest lessons he taught me were about tenacity. He taught me humility and pride in musical accomplishments. To be confident enough to stand on any stage, with any audience - large or small – and engage them, to leave them feeling entertained and with the sense of having been witness to something special. John taught me that there are no limits and to be proud of one's accomplishments.

He also had a perceptive side and quite often showed me a profound intuitive insight. Through all his ups and downs, good times and hard times, he had an ability to see and interpret certain elements of life with absolute clarity. Other times, as with all humans, he stumbled along like a blind man looking for a miracle. One of my favourite "jewels of wisdom" that John left me with was; "Everyone you meet and encounter in life you effect and they affect you. Some we effect in a big way, some in a small way. We may not always know how or why, but we do."

John was tough as nails, although he'd tell you he wasn't. He was hard as rock, but with a tender heart and a self sacrificing, giving attitude that impressed many when he set his mind to a cause. A horse trader and a hustler who knew his limitations and his assets as a musician, as a human being. He criss crossed this country several times playing music and gigging everywhere he went.

Thank you Ike, for honouring my brother John. He was an incredible, colourful man, who was as you said, happiest singing a country song. He was also an incredible brother and mentor.

Theo Massop

THE STORY OF BRONSON'S HARDWARE, ANOTHER LEGENDARY VALLEY BUSINESS!

PN13885

PN90450

Before it was Bronson's, it was Carter's General Store, on Johnston Road. Fred Bronson put his name on the door and added the words "hardware" and "furniture" to the sign, when he purchased Carter's in 1951. He would continue to "grow" the landmark business until 1967, when long-time employee Jack Dunbar bought out the store on June 1, 1967. Jack, who started with Bronson's in 1952, often said the most "memorable" time in the firm's history was when the store was totally destroyed by fire on May 23, 1958.

The business re-opened under the cover of an air supported tent 18 days after the blaze, but a wind storm blew the make-shift structure down, forcing Bronson's to move into the United Church Hall on Elizabeth, until September 7, 1958, when the new store was finished, in the original location.(that building houses several businesses today)

The top picture shows the heart of Alberni's business district that was scarred by fire on May 23, 1958. That picture, which was taken at Elizabeth and Johnston, shows the size of the blaze. You can see the Bank of Commerce was on the corner now occupied by Multi Max, and Alberni Electric was next door where Japhie's Clothing is located today.

The second photo, which was taken from across the street, shows the extent of destruction done to Bronson's and Anderson's Groceteria. Both photos are from the Alberni Museum's collection.

The third picture (from my personal collection) was taken in the mid 70's, and is the image many of us still have of Bronson's when it was known as "the big store with the stock."

ANOTHER READER RESPONDS....

Heather McCulloch e-mailed this response to the 1958 ADHS photo I ran a couple of weeks ago.

"I have sent you a list of names of the people in Mrs. Dino's 1958 Grade 10 class. Found the class photo in my 1959 school annual. Enjoy reading your column "This Was Then".
Thanks Heather.

Here once again is the photo with all the names, some of them you'll recognize I'm sure.

DIVISION 18--BACK ROW: Keith Hunter, Raymond Nass, Don Rewakowsky, Karan Hunter, Edward Hemmingsen, Barrie Williamson , David Lewis, Jack Mitchell, Don Neale. Third Row: John Moan, Sharon Dallman, Judy Plaunt, Celema Mauws, Linda Steele, Jeanette Ekland, Wayne Nickason, Mrs. Dino. Second Row: Sharon Watts, Jan Arnold, Vivian Muldoe, June Holcombe, Frances Dixon, Gail Baldock, Delia Wehle, Lorraine Keller, Beccie Dame. Front Row: Don McCreight, Brodie Hunt. Missing: Dave McLellan, Chuck Crawley, Joan Fink, Dianne Jacobsen.

THE YEAR WAS 1977...

Fletchers Furniture & Appliances was still open downtown. Al Knight was the Manager, and Reg Brooks was one of the sales people. Jean Burns was still open on Third Avenue, The Port Side Inn Restaurant was on Victoria Quay and Port Light House was on Argyle.

Also in 1977, Jack & Doug offered lower prices than Vancouver on the 1978 GLC Mazdas, at BUFFIES at 3rd & Kingsway.

Paula Anderson was the "open line" show host weekdays on CJAV, Scotty's Tire Center was on 6th Avenue, across from the City Works Yard, and Jack was still serving at the J & L Drive-in.

EARTHQUAKE
Sunday, June 23, 1946

The day they felt the earth move in Alberni! I am sure you've heard the stories about the "quake of '46." A lot of folks said that was the reason the old Post Office at Third and Angus was replaced in 1959 and torn down in 1961. Others say that was "bull" and was just an excuse. I say it was unfortunate, but I can also say this " the quake did stop the famous town clock." See for yourself what the June 27, 1946 issue of the West Coast Advocate had to say::

THE TOWN CLOCK STOPPED...

Although the City of Alberni was hard hit by Sunday morning's earthquake Port Alberni escaped serious damage, with exception of two instances—the Post Office tower and the power plant at Bloedel, Stewart & Welch Ltd.

It appears at this time, that the famous town clock has at last petered out after a career of stops and starts. Running on a fairly accurate schedule recently it took an earthquake to put it out of business when the clock tower suffered severe cracks which have made it unsafe. Just what will happen now depends upon inspection by construction men.

The Advocate went on to say that the earth tremor took place at 10:15 am, while the Times Colonist reported it "about 9:30 am." The fact that there were no deaths or accidents reported in the Alberni Valley was attributed to the quake happening on a Sunday morning. At any other time, the report goes on to say, the falling front of the Motion block (see photo below) would have pinned down a number of pedestrians, shoppers and patrons.

(courtesy of my personal collection) This picture, taken just after the quake struck, shows the damage done to the Motion block building, which was torn down a few years ago to make way for the new Golden Dragon restaurant.

MORE ON THE QUAKE THAT WAS FELT FROM VANCOUVER ISLAND TO SEATTLE, and was recorded as far away as West Bromwich Observatory, near Birmingham, England.

The Times Colonist of June 25, 1946, reported Dr. Ernest A. Hodgson, chief of the seismological branch of the department of mines and resources at Ottawa, said the epicentre of the quake was felt throughout most of the Pacific Northwest. It was thought that the quake was on land, and not under the Pacific.

The question asked then was "Why was it not followed by after shocks?" Courtenay, Comox, and Campbell River reported more damage then the Alberni Valley, but here is what the Colonist did say about our area::

According to the report in the Colonist of June 25, 1946: "Alberni was the worst affected community on the west coast. Buildings collapsed, chimneys went either through the roofs, or rolled down the sides tearing off shingles as they went. Walls buckled and the timbers creaked and swayed, terrifying the occupants."

Houses that were on hills or even slight inclines, were in worse condition, than homes on flat ground, especially in the kitchens. Dishes fell out of cupboards, some with such force as to go through windows. Some homes had barely enough unbroken dishes for a meal setting.

The coastal ship Uchuck, on its Sunday trip to Bamfield, also felt the earthquake. One family who had been on the ship at the time, said that it sounded like the ship was running over rocks. The captain stopped the engines while he and the crew looked the ship over for any sign of damage. The shock continued for about a minute. A short time later the ship ploughed through very heavy swells. Navigation lights and buoys along the 35-mile inlet were also damaged.

The Alberni Valley would be shaken by an earthquake three years later, in 1949, then once in 1951, twice in '52 and one I remember feeling in 2001, as I sat at my desk in the showroom at Harbortowne Ford. If you have any photos or memories to share, please contact me through THE PENNYWORTH.

Thanks to The Alberni Valley Historical Society.

A FOLLOW-UP FROM DENMARK....

Remember a few months ago when I wrote about a young man & his wife coming to Port Alberni to trace his father's footsteps from fifty years ago?

Jan Bonde told Linda & I about his dad, Vagn Bonde, who lived here from July, 1951 to August, 1954, and he worked at THE PURITY BAKERY.

Well, we e-mailed the Purity Bakery column to Jan, who showed it to his father. Here's part of the reply we got back on October 19.

"During my dad's stay in Port Alberni the Purity Bakery looked like the picture on the left.(before the awning and front facade was done) The Red Bird Coffee Shop was not located next to the bakery during my dad's stay in town. Unfortunately, he can't remember what was next door, but he has a lot slides which we'll look into. One story from my dad::Working at the bakery, almost every morning the mayor "George" (married to a Swedish woman) and his assistant "Roy", showed up for coffee, before taking off on their freight route. According to my dad, the mayor was delivering packages etc.

We will be hearing more from Jan and his dad, but this information confirms that the renovations to the Purity Bakery were done after August, 1954. That would also mean the Red Bird Coffee Shop was started after that time.

SOMETIMES A GREAT STORY CAN JUST HAPPEN!!

Recently I was rummaging through my personal archives and up popped a scrap of paper that I thought would make an interesting story. Little did I realize then how that one note, which I had saved since 1971, would turn into an even bigger local human interest tale that reached as far as Ottawa. The note was an introduction to the song "Tribute to Canada", written by the late Ann Meister, and recorded in the Valley especially for air-play on CJAV on November 11, 1971. The 3-minute tune was sung by Joseph Ekland, the music was arranged by Yvonne Forbes and the musical accompaniment was provided by Lydia Mueller.

NOW THE STORY GETS MORE INTERESTING... I contacted Ann Meister's son, Felix, who provided me with the facts that his mother's song had reached a number of ears in Ottawa. Felix showed me letters his mother had received from the Prime Minister's office, as early as 1967, which show that she had originally submitted the song as a "Centennial theme" in 1967.

Anne continued to lobby the Feds to use the "Tribute to Canada" tune over the next few years, and with Hugh Anderson's help, she pushed to have the song used during the 1976 Montreal Olympics.

It never was, but the Prime Minister, the Right Honorable Pierre Eliott Trudeau became aware of her pleas. Felix recalls his mother telling him "the only reason the song was not used at the Montreal Olympics in 1976 was that there was no French translation from the original English version. Mr. Warren Allmond told mom that if her song had been used, she would have been invited expense free to Montreal."

Then, when Mr. Trudeau paid a visit to Port Alberni, on May 30, 1976, he met Anne Meister, and heard "a Tribute to Canada," as recited by 11-year old Jean Tetarenko.

It was at the Glenwood Centre, during the Alberni Valley Youth Festival of the Arts, and Barry Miller, who conducted his Eric Dunn School Band that day, recalls the Prime Minister conducting the band through one of their selections. One of the students presented him with an EJ Dunn Band sweater.

In a thank you letter sent to Jean Tetarenko, Jan Peterson, then chairman of the Festival, noted "from all reports, and from my personal observations, Mr. Trudeau really enjoyed himself. He felt among friends and responded accordingly."

Thank you Anne Meister for writing a song that was heard in Ottawa almost 40 years ago. If you have any fond memories of the Trudeau visit 29 years ago, please contact me at the Pennyworth.

Photo courtesy of Jean Tetarenko

Talk about being one up on the Prime Minister. Jean Tetarenko remembers having to stand on a chair to reach the microphone on May 30, 1976, when she recited Anne Meister's "a Tribute to Canada."

It is 1956 – you're at the corner of Johnston & Victoria Quay

T. Allan McLeod stood on one of the most historic corners in the Valley over 50 years ago – and snapped a moment of time with his Brownie Bulls Eye camera.

"I believe it was 1956 when I took these shots of Johnston & Victoria Quay," Allan recalled. "Eddie Allen's garage used to be across the street, a BA service station (where the Liquor Barn is now) when my dad came out of the army in '47 and first worked for Eddie.

At that time, Corfield Motors owned the northwest corner of the intersection at Johnston & Victoria Quay. Eddie bought it in the early 50's and moved his Dodge, Chrysler dealership over then."

When one looks back over the decades (Alberni was incorporated in 1913) and takes into consideration of the millions of tourists heading to the West Coast each year, it's easy to theorize that probably more people have turned the corner of Johnston & Victoria Quay than any other corner in the Valley.

Allan McLeod took this picture of Allen's Super Service (where Pescadores restaurant is now) from across the street.
"That's our '55 Plymouth in front of the pumps," he pointed out. "I think that's a '53 Plymouth on the right."

This shot was taken from in front of the old Alberni City Hall (where the welcoming figures are now).

This photo is slightly blurred but you can still get a good idea of how the corner looked with the Alberni City Hall at the end of Johnston. Allan stood out in the street near the Arlington Hotel as he clicked this one back in 1956.

SPEAKING OF MEN'S WEAR STORES...

You know me. I always like to write about various old businesses that I come across in my archival travels. "Johnny's Men's Wear" was one of the many men's clothing stores that served the Twin Cities back in the '40's to mid-60's.

John M. Rivard opened his business in the middle of October, 1947, in the North side shopping centre, which is what Third Avenue North was called 61 years ago (what we know as lower Third Avenue today). An article in the West Coast Advocate at the time reported:

"This business is located just beyond the Dry Creek Bridge, close to Sowerby Motors. Johnnie is a young man who has recently left college in Gravelbourg, Saskatchewan and has been assisted into business by his father, P.F. Rivard, who has come to Port Alberni to reside."

Now to give you a better idea of where Johnny's Men's Wear (420 3rd Avenue North) actually was, from 1947 to early 1957, it would have been just north of where the DQ is today. Sowerby Motors was on the corner of 3rd and Napier then. In 1958 Leo Katila's Valley Esso Service took over where Sowerby's was.

Harbortowne Ford unveiled new look 17 years ago!

Owner Larry Mallory, Service Manager Tommy McMillan and Parts Manager Rob Johnson pose in front of the newly renovated Harbortowne Ford before the open house in 1992.

The staff of Harbortowne Ford showed off their new renovated facilities to the public on June 26 and 27, 1992. Larry Mallory, who opened the dealership in 1983, hired local architect Lyle Anaka to design a complete makeover and contracted Eric Pardy's construction firm to do the work.

The result – an indoor showroom, redesigned parts & reception area, and a much larger, more efficient shop that was relocated to another part of the building. In other words, not much remained of the original facility, which was home to Ivan Hedman's Alberni Volkswagen for many years.

GONE BUT NOT FORGOTTEN...TENNESSEE ERNIE FORD

The deep-voiced singer who loaded up "SIXTEEN TONS" and climbed to the top of the pop and country music charts in 1955, passed away on October 17, 1991, in Reston, Virginia. He was 72.

It was August 1974....

When Toosha Houle was a winner of Safeway's "Courtesy Contest". Toosha was one of eight Safeway employees who were selected as winners in the contest, which was conducted within Safeway stores throughout B.C. Congratulations again Toosha!

TOOSHA HOULE
Port Alberni

He was "Robbie" Shick, the minor hockey player, in 1974

Rob Shick's NHL referee shirt retired

Rob Shick will be back in town this weekend for the annual Charity Golf Classic, an event he helped organize in 1994. Not only is Rob one of the special guests, along with media personalities, players and former players, but his NHL referee's shirt will be retired following the dinner this Saturday night. Rob's shirt number is 16, he is a 16 handicap and this is the 16th Tourney – what a combination!

That's young Rob Shick (middle) listening as hockey ambassador par-excellence "Babe" Pratt talked shop during a 1974 visit to the old Community Arena. Rob's teammate, Tim Lajeunesse, is getting some advice from Pratt, who was the public relations director for the Vancouver Canucks when he was here on a two-day visit thirty-five years ago.

Cougar Brown info is flowing in...

Since I ran the Cougar Brown picture on July 16, I have received numerous phone calls and emails about the legendary – and mysterious – cougar hunter. Among the many responses, which I am formulating into an upcoming story, was this picture sent in by Cynthia Ammann.

"I remember my parents, Lil and Scotty Ammann, talking about these cougar cubs," Cynthia emailed. "Everybody in Port Alberni knew about them, especially the loggers. You can see by the barn and the dog that it is the same place as the picture published before."

Cynthia found the photo recently among her late mother's things and the only information written on the back was 'Harold Bronson with litter of cougar pups 1943'.

That year makes sense to Cynthia because "My parents were just married and it was before my father went off to the war, so I presume it was the spring/summer of 1943."

Like so many folks who once knew Harry "Cougar" Brown, Cynthia's parents are both gone, but Al Boyko came to see me and I mentioned the name Harold Bronson to him.

"Harold Bronson was the works superintendent at Franklin," he said. "He was killed on the job in the early '50's."

Al and his older brother, Freddie, knew Cougar Brown and I'll be passing on what they recall in that future story.

Pioneer family's youngest child turns 80

This photo was taken almost 60 years ago, at the Darby family farm, at the end of Halpenny Road. "It was taken in 1952 or '53," Jim said. "That's me on the tractor, my brother Ted is up on the load of hay and my dad is standing on the left."

The son of pioneers is now a pioneer himself. Robert James "Jim" Darby turned 80 years old this Tuesday (Sept. 22) and yesterday (Sept. 23) was his 42nd wedding anniversary. His daughter, Heather, thought his story would make for interesting reading, so she approached me with the idea.

"My father has lived in the Valley his entire life and his parents were early pioneers here," she related. "He raised his family on the same piece of property in Beaver Creek where he was raised."

As it turns out, Jim Darby loves to read "This Was Then" each week, so it is even more fitting to wish him a "Happy 80th Birthday" on these pages.

I visited with Jim and his wife of 42 years this Monday out at the historic farm on Halpenny Road where he was born on September 22, 1929. We reminisced in the living room of the Darby farmhouse on the hill, the same spot where the original house, built in 1915 by Jim's father, sat.

"The old house burnt down in 1964," Jim mentioned. "They didn't save much, but no one was hurt. My dad had already passed away by then but my mom, brother Ted and I rebuilt on the same spot."

In 1967, after Jim married Phyllis, he brought her to the farm and raised his own family there.

"The kids have kids of their own now," Jim reflected. "But Phyllis and I are still here, for now."

To my question of what will happen when they can no longer live on their own so far out of town, Phyllis asks "Can you see him in Fir Park?"

But wait a minute! Back to the beginning - Jim was the youngest of four children born to Sydney James "Bob" Darby and Elizabeth "Lizzie" Darby (nee McNeill), both Valley pioneers.

Elizabeth was six years old when her family immigrated to Canada in 1898, first to Cumberland, then a year later coming to Alberni. Her parents settled a small farm out Beaver Creek, in the area that later became the junction of Thompson and Bainbridge Roads.

Jim's father, Sydney or "Bob" as he was known, came from England in the early 1900's. He purchased property from Joe Halpenny and started a farm on Halpenny Road in Beaver Creek.

He married Elizabeth in 1915, took her there as a bride and they lived out their lives there.

"I'm the only one left now," Jim told me. "I never expected to live to see 80, so this is a bonus."

Jim's life hasn't been easy, but his "you go with the times" philosophy has stood him well over the decades.

"We always had something to eat through the "dirty thirties" and I remember the black outs during the war years. I just missed going in the army but when I was old enough I joined the Rangers locally. I bought my 30-30 carbine for five dollars after and used that for hunting for about ten years. I only went as far as Grade 8 in school because there was no bus transportation to town then."

Jim has been a farm hand for most of his life. The family had dairy cows at one time, even went into raising beef cattle later on.

He "hayed" for farms all over the Valley for a long time, quitting just last year.

"I also drove truck for Bob Mills, then Rayner & Bracht, retiring on June 30, 1990," Jim offered. "My health has been pretty good until this year."

So now, the oldest member of the Alberni District Co-op (his dad was a founding member and Jim inherited Bob's number 65) plans to do very little, besides the dishes and drive his wife to town that is.

"I canned tomatoes the other day," Jim proclaimed.

Happy 80th Birthday Mr. Robert James "Jim" Darby, and many more. It was a real pleasure meeting you and an honour writing about you!

P.S. Happy Birthday to Phyllis who is younger than you are today (Sept. 24).

More Cougar Brown memories

Ken Beaupit emailed recently to say that he knew Cougar Brown quite well.

"I looked after his blue tick hounds while he was in Port Alberni hospital with his heart attack," Ken wrote. "I knew him in the early 70's while working for McMillan Bloedel in the forestry department. I would drive by his cabin almost daily in the crummy on my way to work with my fellow workers. He once had 17 blue tick hounds at one time, while I was there, there were 11 of them, the oldest being Matilda who was blind and barely managed to walk. I remember I wouldn't lay on the couch because of the piles of dog hair. I sat and slept in the easy chair beside the stove."

Ken also recalls Cougar Brown's homemade saki and beer.

"He used to cold smoke his salmon, never tasted anything like it," Ken added. "Cougar Brown used to pan for gold almost every day in China Creek, I accompanied him on this excursion one time."

And – longtime resident Chuck Johnston still has fond memories of "Cougar", as he referred to Cougar Brown. Chuck, who first came to the Valley in 1946, worked at Camp 1, Sarita River, then out to Ucluelet, returning to Port Alberni in 1967.

"One day in the 70's, I saw Cougar at Woodward's store," Chuck related to me on the phone. "He asked me for a ride home and along the way out to his cabin, he asked me to stop at the corner store on Anderson Avenue, where he bought a brick of banana ice cream, which he fed to his dogs as a treat."

Chuck remembers Cougar using a big spoon to give each dog in turn some ice cream.

"He never bothered ever taking any pictures," Chuck said. "And he didn't like hippies, any guys with long hair."

After working for Jack McKay for 17 years, Chuck retired in 1987, but he still lives in town and he still remembers "Cougar".

This 1948 picture of Lee Donovan, left, and Bob Cowley, was taken out at the McLean Mill, where they both worked at the time. Check the size of the bearskin on the left.

You cannot write about cougar hunters in the Valley and not talk about the legendary hunting skills of the late Bob Cowley, so I will have his remarkable story in the months ahead.

For those of you that didn't know Bob, who sadly passed away on October 3, 2000, here is a small part of what Diane Dobson wrote after interviewing him for his life story back in 1999.

"Since the age of eight years, Bob Cowley was out hunting and trapping with his dad. As an 11-year old, he shot his first deer. Throughout his life, Bob hunted both for meat and for bounty. Cougar hunting was for bounty. Bob shot his first at the age of 15 years in the mountains back of Creelman's farm. Even before that, Bob had been cougar hunting with his dad but this was the first he bagged.

It wasn't until 1945, that Bob was heavily into bounty hunting. He was making $20.00 per cougar. Then, under contract with the government, the price went up to $40.00. For this fee, the hunters were required to hunt what were considered 'nuisance' cougars. These were animals causing havoc on farms and in residential areas. Other cougar hunters, men well known to Bob, were Harry 'Cougar' Brown, Jack Wilson and Red Larson. The highest rate of pay Bob received for killing a nuisance cougar was $150.00. Like his father, Bob shot the first and last cougar at this high rate of pay. This was much later, in the 1980's."

Class of '55 host a mid-week 55-year reunion Sept. 8 and 9

A group of 1955 high school graduates who still live in Port Alberni or nearby have met and arranged to celebrate the 55th anniversary of their departure from grade 12.

"We have organized a casual two-day event, which will take place on Wednesday, and Thursday, September 8 and 9," remarked Marilyn Horton (Fox), a member of the reunion committee. "We have chosen this date because it falls between the annual Salmon Festival and the Fall Fair. We thought that our out-of-town guests might be interested in attending one or both of these events as well as the reunion."

An afternoon social and dinner is planned at the Alberni Golf Club on the Wednesday, and as at past reunions, the Redford's will be hosting a brunch at their Sproat Lake home on the Thursday.

If you are planning to attend, please return your registration form as soon as possible, or at least contact Marilyn at: mhorton@shaw.ca or at 250-723-7640.

"About fifty have responded so far," Marilyn reported. "We even have one of our former teachers coming. Miss Hunkin (now Machan) has indicated she will be here."

Those students who would have, or should have, graduated in 1955, but for some reason did not, are also welcome.

It's hoped that a trip down memory lane, in the form of a tour of ADSS (ADHS back then), will also take place sometime over the two-day reunion. Regardless, all those who attend will undoubtedly have plenty to reminisce about since their Graduation Exercises on Friday, June 3, 1955.

These 1955 ADHS Graduates are among those who will be returning Sept. 8 and 9

Dagmar Back

Marilyn Fox

Dave Osborne

Robert "Bert" Ward

Recalling the 1971 Alberni Athletic Wanderers soccer team

George Glaser was the coach of the Wanderers back in 1971 when this picture was taken.

"They were quite the team," George proudly proclaimed. "I thought folks might like see the players again 39 years later."

George has provided the names, except for one. If you can put a name to the fourth face from the left in the back row, or you have memories to share, please contact me at: ikepatterson@telus.net

Front Row – (left to right): Les Sam, Danny Olsen, Louis Biresak, Tony Powell, Peter Glaser and Craig Mathews.

Back Row – (left to right): Wayne Deforrest, Ted Roberts, Dave McMurdle, Leo Van Vliet, ____, Brian Cairney and Seigi Christl.

Oldtimers will love this rare picture from Gerry Hickford

"I came across this picture (from my father-in-law's collection)," Gerry emailed on September 28, 2009. "This was Benny's Dine and Dance, located about where Regina and Johnston Road is today. It was taken in June 1949 and it was where my sister-in-law's reception was held that year. My own wedding reception was also held at Benny's in August 1950."

Another story from the back burner files
Amanda Irg remembers when Miss Canada came to town in 1984

"I saw your story in the Feb. 25 edition in regards to Feb. 1984 – Miss Canada spends busy two days here," Amanda Irg emailed back on April 14. "Granny Irene Manton was my grandmother. I remember that day very well (Saturday, Feb, 11, 1984 when Miss Canada, Cynthia Kereluk, walked in the annual Grammathon for the Variety Club). Us kids beat our drums all the way up Johnston Road to the mall. Did I mention it was raining..(lol).

Irene Manton and her husband Don were instrumental in getting Miss Canada to come to Port Alberni twenty-six years ago. They personally paid the airfare from Toronto for Miss Canada and a chaperone.

"She also did the first rubber ducky race in Roger Creek Park," Amanda recalled about her Granny Irene. "We always did Bowl for Kids, I even went on the Variety Club Telethon to donate the money we raised with her. Irene was a community-minded lady and did some amazing things. I'm glad I got to share in some of that with here. She is missed dearly."

Young Amanda Irg (on the right of Miss Canada) was one of the little drummers who took part in the 1984 Grammathon from Victoria Quay to the Alberni Mall. Do you know the names of Amanda's drum-mates who are in this photo with Cynthia Kereluk (Miss Canada)?

Rose Annette Paquette becomes Miss Alberni Valley 1971

During the two-week period leading up to the 1971 pageant, Rose Annette Paquette represented the J & L Drive-in. Then, on Saturday, May 8, she left the ADSS Auditorium as the new Miss Alberni Valley. As history has recorded, the 17 year-old was composed and smiling as she walked to the microphone to accept the honour, but dissolved in tears as she faced the audience.

Other candidates gathered around to comfort and congratulate Rose Annette, including Maureen McKinnon, Miss Plaza Shopping Centre, who was given the title of first princess; and Maureen Hamagishi, Chamber of Commerce representative, second princess.

Retiring after her year as Miss Alberni Valley, Laura Gregory was overcome by emotion and cried into the microphone. Junior Chamber of Commerce president Leroy Loewen relieved the tension when he presented a bucket to catch the tears, and according to news reports, "the evening closed in a scene of jubilation as the new Miss Alberni Valley was crowned."

Seconds after being announced as the new Miss Alberni Valley 1971, Rose Annette Paquette, is the centre of attention on stage in the ADSS Auditorium. Here she is surrounded, from left to right, by retiring princess Leah Grinwis, 1970 Miss A.V. Laura Gregory, and Miss Kinsmen Donna Roberts.

RIGHT: Miss Alberni Valley Rose Annette Paquette with her attendants, Maureen Hamagishi, left, and Maureen McKinnon, at the 1971 pageant.

A fiery moment for P. A.'s first fire boat

The exact details surrounding this picture of Port Alberni's original Frank Harrison fire boat (replaced in 1977) in action are sketchy. I've had the photo, believed taken in 1967, for a while, waiting for the right moment to publish it. Now that the MV Frank Harrison II is also out of service – and out of the water, literally – I felt this was the right time to show it. Anyone with more information about this picture can email me at: ikepatterson@telus.net

By the way, the first Frank Harrison fire boat was sold to Bamfield after it was retired in 1977. As of press time this week, there have been no bidders on the Frank Harrison II. Anyone interested can contact Port Alberni Fire Chief Tim Pley for details.

Goodbye to the Frank Harrison II

The MV Frank Harrison II sits on dry land last Saturday morning after being on call with the Port Alberni Fire Department for 33 years. With the popular fire boat as it takes retirement are, left to right, Firefighter Travis Cross, Firefighter Rick Newberry, Captain Al Carroll (Retired), Fire Chief Tim Pley, Deputy Fire Chief Chris Jancowski and Firefighter Andre Guerin. [PA Fire Dept. photo]

It happened in August

It was early August 1975 when these young musicians hesitated to strike up a tune because of the poor soundproofing in the Gyro Youth Centre's basement. The trio joined the then campaign for noise muffing materials to line the band room walls. From left, Rick Znidarsic, Wayne Coulson and Marty McMillan used the basement room as a place to practise, and in return they played for youth dances and offered guitar and drum lessons for interested teens.

Can you hear me now?

Hear ye, hear ye, sayeth the Town Crier as he demonstrates his communications skills to Mayor Jim Robertson on Thursday, June 29, 1978. The town crier was Alfie Howard, an honest-to-goodness Cockney and official town crier of the Greater London Borough of Lambeth and the Isle of Wight. Brought to Canada as a Woodward's Store promotion, Alfie was touring B.C. and Alberta. He brought Good Greetings to the mayor of Port Alberni from the mayor of Lambeth.

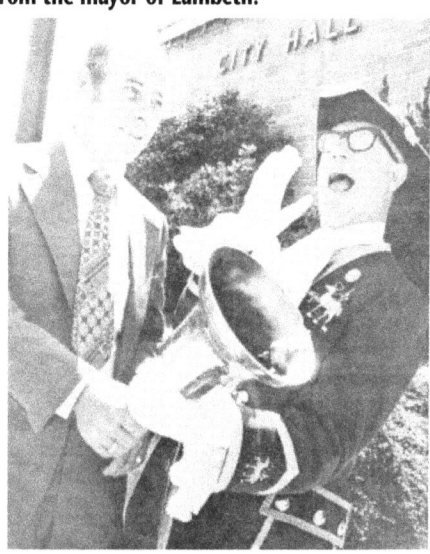

On August 29, 1973 the retiring manager of Port Alberni theatres, Robert Gordon Lyall (left), introduced John Bishop of Victoria who will take over the position in early fall. Mr. Lyall and his wife Rose managed the local theatres since May 1947, when Famous Players took over the old Port Theatre of Harold Warren on First Avenue. They planned to enjoy retirement in their summer home near Sooke.

Does this picture look familiar to you?

Port Alberni's Kevan van Herd took this photo of the "piling forest" which was driven to support the Number 3 and 4 paper machines in the mid-fifties construction at Alpulp (now Catalyst Paper of course). You'll notice the highway went along the Somass River at that time. The Hydro substation (in the same place today) is clearly visible in the upper right side of the picture. The construction camp is off to the right of that. If you look hard enough, using a magnifying glass helps, you'll see some houses on the river bank north of Roger Creek (those disappeared during the 1964 tidal wave).

A nice story is still a nice story – even if it is 25 years old

Public criticism about living in Port Alberni (not always constructive) seems to be going around during these economic hard times. In some cases, individuals enjoy "bashing" everything that happens, or does not happen here. After living here for the past 44 years, I can tell you that life in this city - and the greater community – is not that bad. Over the years, countless visitors and new residents have confirmed this fact. This nice story about Port Alberni appeared in the AV Times on Monday, Dec. 8, 1986:

A motoring Saskatchewan couple believes Port Alberni must be a nice place to live. On Saturday, Nov. 15, Jack and Alice Greening of Christopher Lake, Sask. were trying to make the ferry driving from Tofino. Their car broke down west of Sproat Lake.

"Many motorists stopped and offered help while we waited for the tow truck," the couple wrote the Times.

But the story gets even better for the couple.

"We were taken to the home of the tow truck driver and fed banana cream pie while we waited for the diagnosis of our trouble from the garage owner. Who had been called out after hours, by an RCMP corporal who was also off-duty.

We were given the use of a car to take our daughter to the ferry so she wouldn't miss work the next day and so that we could keep a breakfast date in Courtenay the next morning."

The couple told this story of what they considered "extraordinary kindness" and were surprised by the response.

"The comments were 'that's the way they are in Port Alberni,'" the Greenings wrote the Times to tell their story because "we wanted to say thanks again."

All of which should be enough for the community named the one with a heart to take another bow – this time for friendliness.

Sunday, Nov. 15, 1987 – P.A. Salmondoes strike at Campbell River's reputation

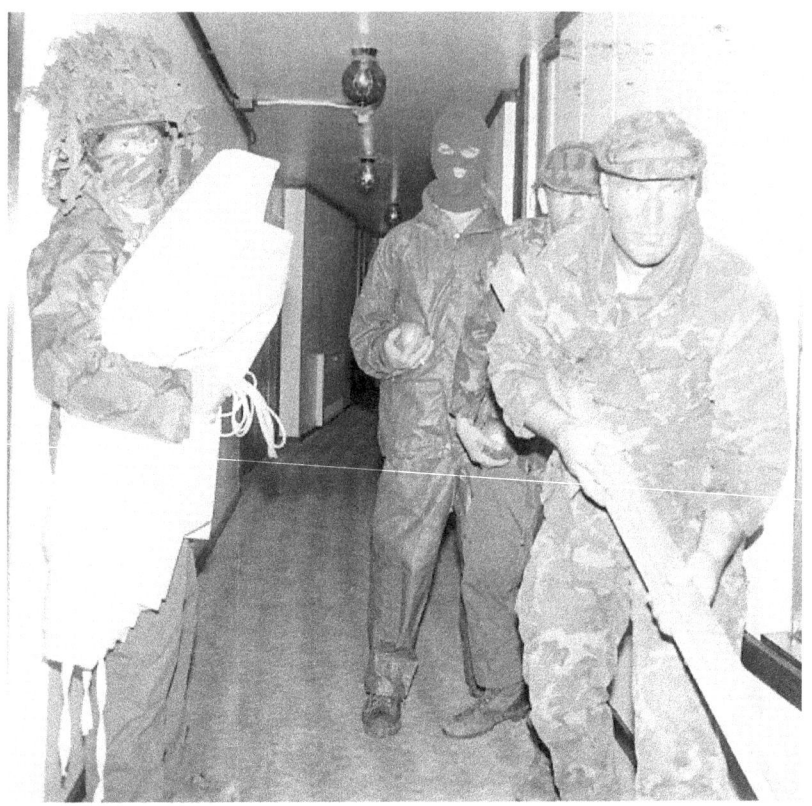

It was during the days when being "Salmon Capital of the World" was more than just a war of words between Port Alberni and Campbell River. As the story goes - reaction followed action starting in the spring of 1987 when the Salmondoes hung a banner on the old Chamber of Commerce building in the north Island town. That was followed by two attempts on the part of Campbell River to change the record. Unknown persons staged a banner ceremony in Port Alberni during Labour Day weekend 23 years ago. However, it backfired when the paper banner had the word 'salmon' spelled incorrectly. The banner was draped at Alberni Harbour Quay, instead of Clutesi Haven Marina, but when the spelling mistake was found, the Port Alberni Salmon Festival Society had the banner moved to Clutesi for the eyes of B.C., via the media telecasting the event, to see for themselves how little Campbell River really knew about salmon.

Then that September, Campbell River tried flying helium filled balloons with an advertisement proclaiming it the Salmon Capital. Prevailing winds blew the balloons north over Campbell Lake, however, instead of south where the message might have meant something in terms of publicity.

As history has recorded, the claim of being the Salmon Capital of the World has seesawed between the two communities ever since. However, now that Port Alberni is "The Ultimate Fishing Town in Canada", the time has come to give up the battle for bragging rights to that worn-out title that just refers to salmon fishing. After all, ultimate means "greatest possible".

Top: The Salmondoes, a self-styled local salmon terror squad, creep down the hall of the Discovery Inn, at 6 a.m. on Sunday, Nov. 15, 1987, on the way to their jump-off point for an assault on Campbell River's reputation as salmon capital of the world.

Bottom: Once on the roof, the 4-man crew assembles support for the 40-foot banner, and at right, in the pre-dawn light the banner proclaims Port Alberni as the new Salmon Capital of the World.

The Salmondoes daring assault had short-lived glory though, because by 8 a.m. the banner had been discovered and removed by Discovery Inn staff.

Talk about hard times, go back to October 1981

OK Tires and Western Motors were two of the visible victims of the economic slump in the Valley back in October 1981.

Twenty-nine years ago today (Oct. 28) the Alberni Valley was swimming in a sea of economic uncertainty. In fact, many local businesses claimed it was the worst they had ever seen.
The layoffs of hundreds of MacMillan Bloedel mill workers, combined with the high cost of borrowing money, sent shock waves throughout the Valley economy, forcing businesses to lay off staff or simply close up shop. Anyone who lived here back in October 1981 can undoubtedly remember the businesses that fell by the wayside and those who were rumoured to be on the brink of bankruptcy. OK Tires (located where Alberni Glass is today) and Western Motors (the home of the Pin Cushion and Port Auto Tech now) were two of the noticeable victims. Zellers, then at Third and Angus, announced they would be closing the doors at the end of January 1982. Alberni Cycle and Ski, the local Honda dealership that employed three workers, folded up after nine years on Third Avenue and moved to Nanaimo.
As reported in the AV Times on Oct. 28, 1981;
Leo Katila, of the Chev Olds dealership, says he hasn't seen things so bad since he opened shop in 1961. Plans for a gala 20th birthday party for Katila Motors have been shelved, he said, because "we're not in any mood to celebrate." Expecting a "long, cold winter," Katila predicts it will be spring before local retailers will see an upswing, but perhaps two years before business returns to last year's levels. His own shop has laid off three employees in the face of a 30 per cent drop in business.
Neale Pennington, president of Chatwin Motors, says he has heard the rumors that his 36-year-old dealership is close to receivership but laughs off the possibility. "We've had two red months, but they were not that serious. Other than that, we've made money," he says. Although sales are off 25 per cent, he has not laid off any staff.
Woodward's manager Bill Patenaude is adamant his store will remain open. "Woodward's does not close stores," he says. "If the whole town folds up then of course we'll have to go too. But as long as there's any hope left at all we're staying." Declining to name specific figures, Patenaude says sales of big ticket items are "substantially down, but we're not hurting any worse than any other retailer in town."
Bob Haynes, manager of Jack's Intertruck, also denies rumors his business is headed for receivership but adds the local situation is the worst he has seen in 20 years. Intertruck does work for MacMillan Bloedel and small logging operations. Haynes neatly sums up why he has been forced to lay off 12 staff members.
"If the logging companies aren't working, they're not buying. And if they're not buying, we're not selling," he says.
There are currently 3,380 active claims for unemployment insurance in Port Alberni, more than double the figures for the same time last year, Gus Barrett, manager of the Canada Employment Centre says. This is the most he has seen in the nine years he has been here.
Terry McFadden, district supervisor of the Human Resources Branch, estimates welfare claims are up 20 per cent since August.
Personally, I recall the hardships faced by local retailers 29 years ago, because I was dealing with businesses of all types in my advertising sales position at CJAV. While this was the beginning of the end for some Valley businesses, it was also the dawning of a new era for others. Some trimmed and managed to survive for a period of time, but others reinvented themselves and remained in the market place, until selling out or retiring years later.
For the record – two things are important to note. Although the economic downturn was evident locally at the end of 1981, many business still ended the year in the black. For others, 1980 was the last of the banner years. The ones, who refused to believe the good times of the past would never be back, suffered the most. I witnessed many owners and staff re-dedicating themselves to the business basics of service, selection and competitive pricing in order to keep the doors open. Looking back now, one can easily see how the world's economic woes reached over the hump in 1981, starting a crisis here that the Valley has never – and possibly may never – recover. It has forced everyone, not only businesses, to diversify the way we think and live.

Rare picture discovered, saved and now shared with everyone

Anita Haase brought in a scanned version of the above picture with an equally interesting story.

"My father, Ewald Haase, bought the house at 501 8th Avenue South in 1954 and fixed it up," Anita explained. "He found the 11 x 17 inch picture in the attic and kept it. He loved it and even took it with him when he moved into Fir Park Village."

The year "1908" was written on the back of the picture, which shows the waterfront area of what would become the city of Port Alberni (incorporated in 1912).

"We lived in that house until about 1968," Anita recalled. "My dad kept it as a rental until selling it years later. He was a carpenter at the Pulp Mill."

Anita lost her mother Anna in 1990, and Ewald passed away almost a year ago, on New Year's Eve.

"He loved Port Alberni, often saying how much the mountains reminded him of Germany," Anita added.

Time falls back one hour this weekend

I'm using this 1985 photo as a reminder that Daylight Saving Time officially ends at 2 a.m. this Sunday (Nov. 7), so remember to set your clocks BACK one hour to Pacific Standard Time when you go to bed on Saturday night. Ron Paulson was the acting manager at the Harbour Quay twenty-five years ago and it was his job to change the most visible timepiece in the Valley back then. Today, Ron works at the Multiplex but don't worry, city staff will make sure the tower clock is "back" on time.

Thanks Ike

It is nice when This Was Then items go beyond their sentimental and historical value. Port Alberni's Fire Chief Tim Pley emailed his thanks for running the piece on the retirement and sale of the MV Frank Harrison II (TWT Oct. 21).

"As you know, we advertised the retired fire boat for sale, posting our ad across the province," Tim wrote. "There were no bids received. After your article was published, my phone rang off the wall. We now have several interested parties. Thank you for making that happen Ike."

Over 4,000 turned out for Golden Oldies Peoples Choice Car Show and Demolition Derby April 19 - 20, 1986

There were 20 bleachers packed with spectators for the demolition derby 24 years ago during the Golden Oldies second annual People's Choice Car Show. Over 4,000 car enthusiasts attended the two-day event – the car show in the Glenwood Centre and the demolition derby on the fall fair grounds.

If you were there on April 19 or 20 (maybe both days) you probably put a ballot in for Dan and Georgina Cyr because their 1932 Chev coup won the People's Choice award as the most popular automobile in the show. The Cyrs also placed third in the voting done by the spectators with a 1957 Chev convertible.

A Vancouver man Fred Welsh, who drove over from the mainland in a 1932 Ford Roadster, won the people's second choice.

As reported back then, the Golden Oldies Car Club discovered their demolition derby was just as popular as the first year. The crowds thoroughly enjoyed the smoke, steam and sensational crashes each day, especially when the ladies got behind the wheel. Val Cyr took the Powder Puff Domestic heat on the Saturday, with Anita Bose taking the domestic class on Sunday. Lois Rogers won the Powder Puff Imports heat on Sunday in car number 10 ½.

Dec. 13, 1973 – Russell Park dedicated

Parks and Recreation Commission chairman Bill Gibson, right, presents Dunc Russell with a burl plaque commemorating his service and the renaming of Tenth Avenue Park. The sign with Russell's name on it was designed and constructed by the Vancouver Parks department. Russell began his career in recreation in New Westminster.

It was known as Tenth Avenue Park until Dec. 13, 1973, when it was renamed Russell Park in honour of Dunc Russell, the architect of Port Alberni's recreation program.

"The renaming of the park was adopted unanimously by both the city council and the parks and rec commission, in recognition of Russell's achievement since coming to Port Alberni in March, 1963," Bill Gibson, commission chairman at the time, told those gathered at Echo Centre.

Mayor Fred Bishop kidded Russell about the renaming, saying "I have been after you for years to come up with a more imaginative name for Tenth Avenue park, but since you never got around to it, we had to do it ourselves." He then expressed the sorrow of council in losing a man of Russell's qualifications, but acknowledged, "He has made his mark in Port Alberni."

Russell himself was visibly moved by the ceremonies and said he was "deeply pleased by the sincere appreciation of my 10 year's work here." He spoke at length about the support he had received from staff members, the commission and city council and congratulated Mayor Bishop in particular for "the inspired political direction you have given this community."

Russell continued to work at Echo Centre three days a week until his replacement, Larry Beres of Saskatoon, arrived in early January. He then took up full time duties at a new job in Oak Bay.

Reach for the Top was here in 1975

Terry Garner, the popular host of "Reach for the Top", the CBC TV high school quiz show was in Port Alberni 36 years ago, along with his entire production crew. The Vancouver Island competition was videotaped at the ADSS Auditorium from March 10 to 13. Unfortunately, Port Alberni's Reach for the Top team, which consisted of Dave McKelvey, Sandy Ribeyre, Stephen Balogh and Berry Reumkens, went down to defeat on March 12, during the taping of a semi-final Island zone game. They were beaten by about 100 points by Courtenay's George P. Vanier School. Were you in the audience back then?

You could be in this picture – if you were at Maquinna School in 1973

This photo, which appeared in the AV Times on May 22, 1973, shows a group of Maquinna School students arriving back in Port Alberni on the Lady Rose after attending a camp-out at Bamfield's Brady's Beach. Did you make the voyage down and back 38 years ago?

Over 200 people turned out for Robbie Burns night in 1988
This year's celebrations are scheduled for Saturday, January 22

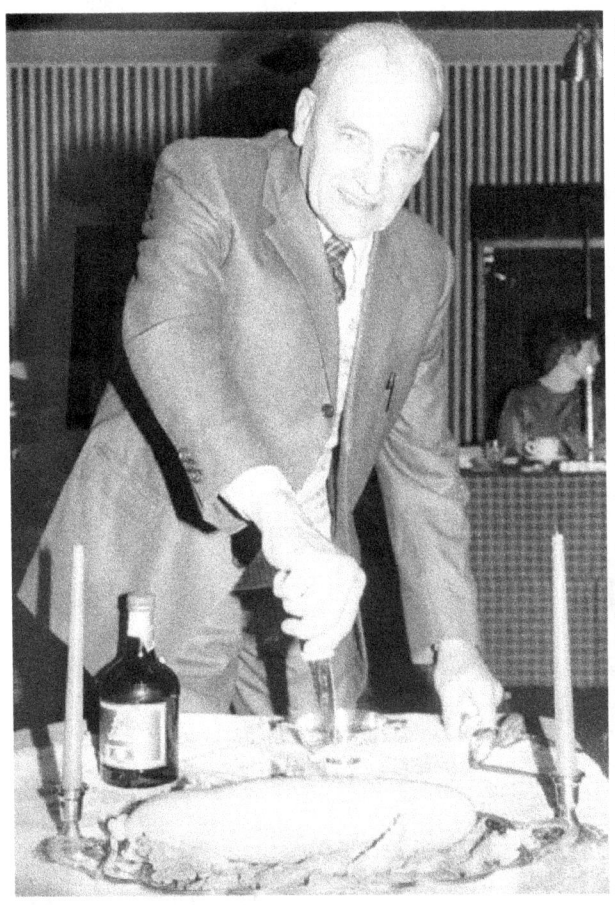

Dan Connell wielded the dirk to do the traditional Haggis honours during the Port Alberni Highland Dancers Association's fifth annual celebration of Robbie Burns night at the Italian Canadian Centre on Saturday, Jan. 23, 1988. Over 200 people came for the "roastit beef and chappit tawties" dinner along with the traditional and contemporary dancing.

This year, the Highland Dancers Association will host their 28th annual Robbie Burns Supper next Saturday, Jan. 22, at the Italian Hall. Tickets are $25 each and are available at Somass Drugs or Echo Centre. The ever-popular Roast Beef dinner, catered by Dave's Catering, will be complimented by performances of the Scottish Country Dancers, the Highland Dancers and the West Coast Highlanders Pipe and Drum Band. As usual, the celebration of the life of Robbie Burns, Scotland's national poet, who died in 1796, will see the legendary Haggis piped in and addressed (tasting is optional).

Recalling 1987 Totem Princess

Congratulations to Samm Moore (female hockey representative) for winning the Totem Spirit award at last weekend's 56th annual Totem Basketball Tournament. Twenty-four years ago, the Totem Princess was Senior Basketball's Karen Dowling. She was chosen as the representative of the club putting the most work into the Totem Tournament and was crowned at half-time on Saturday, Jan. 31, 1987. Flanking Karen then were Gwen Parker (student council), Tracy Johnston (yearbook), Kim Kirkpatrick (Jr. Basketball), and Liette Lehtonen (CounterAttack).

Happy "Big 30" for Fir Park Village

It took a whole community to build a village – Fir Park Village – that opened on Jan. 26, 1981 (official opening was on March 7). Walter Behn, then a city alderman and tireless advocate for the new facility, gave a short history of Fir Park Village.

"The beginnings occurred in 1967 when a local couple, husband 91 and wife 89, were no longer capable of keeping house," he recalled. "The husband found space in a White Rock intermediate care home; his wife in Victoria. The Labour Council made a decision that we would do everything in our power to build an intermediate care home in Port Alberni."

It took two changes of government in Victoria and another 14 years before the project became a reality. Behn said it was not always easy.

"It was a long and it was a thorny road," he told reporters on Jan. 28, 1986. "The Labour Council deserves the credit for the years I put in lobbying for the home."

Sadly, Walter Behn never lived to see the tenth anniversary of Fir Park. He passed away in December 1990. However, he will be in the thoughts of everyone at the upcoming 30th anniversary celebration, along with the late Ken Hutcheson, Henry Nedergard and George McKnight, three of the many other socially conscious individuals who worked hard to see Fir Park Village realized.

Port Boat House follow-up

You may have seen this picture of the original Port Boat House on these pages quite some time ago. Keith Rodgers had sent it my way with the belief that "it was taken in the late 50's or very early 60's." Bob Cole saw the 1962 item about the Port Boat House in last week's column and dropped the photo off again.

"The Port Boat House building you see here would have been where the Donut Shop is now," Bob revealed. "The boat ramp came out where Columbia Fuels used to be."

Newcomers to the Valley have to visualize the foot of Argyle Street without the Harbour Quay (which opened in August 1984).

Old businesses – gone but not forgotten

People still talk about THE BRITE SPOT, regarded as the first drive-in restaurant in the Valley. Like the ad, from the April 30, 1958 Twin Cities Times says, it was located on Beaver Creek Road, next to the Gill School (where Arbutus RV is now). Long-time residents will also recall that a year and a half after this ad appeared, on Nov. 26, 1959, the late Don Gunn and his partners opened the new LANTERN INN on the Brite Spot property. The original Lantern Inn, started on lower Third Avenue in 1956, was destroyed in a fire on August 10, 1959.

This classic ad for the legendary THREE SISTERS CAFÉ was in the West Coast Advocate on Thursday, March 28, 1946.

Do you remember seeing this car around town in 1987?

This car drew a lot of attention 24 years ago when four unidentified youths "created" it out of a 1971 Ford LTD.
The four cut off the roof, and spent about four months working weekends on painting the car.
"The theme is the good times of summer, our last chance to go crazy," they told reporters on July 24, 1987 (when the pictures appeared in the AV Times). "The plan is to drive to the Kelowna Regatta in this car."
Does anyone know if that trip ever happened? Who really owned the car? One youth told the reporter it was his, another said it was his dad's, who didn't know the present condition of the car.
"We used to have a bear skin rug in the trunk, with the head sticking out, but someone in Nanaimo cut the head off," they remarked. "Pretty rude, huh?"
If you remember any details about the attention getting "good times" car of 1987, please share at: ikepatterson@telus.net

More Franklin River memories

This rare picture from Don Watt's father's Franklin River collection shows the Bridge Building crew hard at work in Bear S**t Canyon back in 1939.

Jacquie Bjornson (nee Harris), who grew up in Franklin River's Camp B, discovered this 1952 May Day picture, probably taken by her mother, Pat Harris.
"That's Doug Richmond in the kilt," she told Don Watt, who brought the photo in for me. "I believe that's me with the patch over one eye, on the decorated tricycle."

Horseplay - Port Alberni style

There was plenty of action and a lot of laughter on Sunday, Feb. 18, 1973 when members of the Alberni Riding and Hunt Club saddled up for a game of broomball on horseback. The late Willie Salisbury, left, of the Riders Club and Cyndi Boudreau of the Hunt Club were caught by the Times photographer as they were zeroing in on the ball. The Hunt Club won the game 5-4 in overtime. There were no scoring details provided and the location of the battle wasn't mentioned when this picture appeared in the paper 38 years ago.

Hats off to the woodworkers

Thirty-eight years ago an article ran in the AV Times about the changes made to that date in the fashionable head gear worn by MB employees. "Hard Hats" had been required equipment in the forest industry for many years by the time (Jan. 31, 1973), but many old-timers could still remember the days of the "bonedries."

"In the beginning workers bought their own safety hats," the article reported. "But under the current IWA contract the headgear is supplied by employers and the new model, an Australian import of non-fading orange colour, lighter in weight and strong enough to meet Workmen's Compensation Board's rigid standards, is now being distributed among MB employees in this district.

"The bright orange color is an important safety factor," the company's safety manager Len Kingman added.

Alvin Brown with the old bone-dry.

Jack James models a snappy aluminum hard hat.

John Allen in the original hardboiled model.

Stan Rukin shows the latest in hardhats.

If you were a member of the Community Youth Choir in 1981 – you could be in this picture

Robin Mitchell directs the Community Youth Choir in this picture, which appeared in the AV Times on Friday, February 27, 1981.

It happened in 1975

K-40 member Mayor Howard McLean (squatting left) aided provincial Kinsmen governor Bob deClarke of Port Alberni in planting a tamarack seedling near the Kinsmen Hut at the fall fair grounds on Saturday, August 9, 1975. Incoming local Kinsmen president Hal Bonora, holding the shovel, looks on, together with Kinsmen representatives from all over B.C.

Do you recall when Port Alberni hosted a two-day meeting of Kinsmen representatives from all 10 zones in the province? It was August 9 and 10, 1975. The event included a unique eight-hour business session on the Saturday, on five small boats down the Alberni Inlet.

"We took this opportunity to discuss progress on a peaceful, one-to-one basis," provincial governor Bob deClarke commented. "We switched over every hour, and even caught one fish!"

The day ended at the Kin Hut where the local Kinsmen and Kinettes hosted a steak barbecue for their guests. Port Alberni Mayor Howard McLean was on hand to welcome the visitors, and later helped in a tree-planting ceremony outside the hut. The tree, a tamarack from Prince Albert, Saskatchewan, embodied the 1975 Kinsmen theme of "watch the tree grow while we grow." Each of Canada's district governors was given one of these trees by their national executive.

Sunday's business meeting ratified the district executive's actions to date and also established guidelines for the 1975-76 Kinsmen programs. It was reported that the weekend ended in a mood of eagerness to tackle the year's goals – an improved public relations program and membership drive.

By the way, the Port Alberni Kinsmen and Kinettes will be hosting the District 5 Kinvention this year.

"We're expecting up to 200 visitors from B.C. and the Yukon on the May long weekend," Steve Kalugin reported.

How much was this doggy in the window 41 years ago?

People have commented that I never feature old pictures of dogs on these pages, so here's one, from August 5, 1970. Times' photographer, Roy Snikkers (always had a camera with him) was strolling the downtown area and caught a curious Laddie wanting to see what was going on. Does anyone recognize Laddie? Who owned the truck he was guarding that day? Lets chat at: ikepatterson@telus.net

Bill Patenaude retires in February 1984

Over my years in the Alberni Valley, I have introduced many people and many people have introduced me countless times. It was during one introduction that I was called "a true friend of the community", meaning someone who deeply cares about Port Alberni. That was a label I was proud to be tagged with and in my "lifetime" here I have met many others, who in my opinion, would also qualify to wear the title.

Bill Patenaude was one of those people. I met Bill shortly after arriving in the Valley in 1967 (he came in 1965). After hearing I was from Squamish, he informed me that he had lived in Britannia Beach, and that I would thoroughly enjoy Port Alberni for as long as I stayed here. He was right.

Those of you who have been in the Valley for some time will remember Bill Patenaude from Woodward's. He worked as appliance manager from '65 to '74 before becoming store manager. Others will recall Bill for his involvement with the Alberni Valley Lions Club, South Port Business Association and the Chamber of Commerce.

Bill Patenaude, manager of Woodward's Port Alberni store, retired on February 29, 1984, after serving the company for 30 years.
"I plan to just wake up each morning and let the day take care of itself," Bill told reporters in early November 1983 when he announced his retirement and that Joe Van Bergen would be replacing him. "There is a lot of B.C. and Canada I haven't seen yet." This picture (from the Nov. 4/83 AV Times) shows Bill beside a map of the expanded Woodward's operation in Western Canada.

A 25-year old "Museum Moment"

It was during an evening reception at the Museum on Thursday, January 16, 1986 that Mayor Gillian Trumper unveiled a mural chronicling our history. "A History of Work", a 16-foot long by three feet wide work of art by local artist Elizabeth Stuef shows the history of the Alberni Valley from the earliest days of primitive civilization to the industrial centre that we evolved into. "It is a rare opportunity for an artist to be able to speak at the unveiling of a major piece of their own art," Stuef commented at the reception, which drew an audience of over 80 people. "I have learned a lot about the early days of Port Alberni during my nine-month assignment."

Mayor Trumper said the mural, commissioned by the museum, "is something the Valley will treasure for years."

More on the West Coast Cleaners Story....

The phone has been ringing since I ran the photos of West Coast Cleaners, on Margaret Street, in the '40's. Tony Souchuk called to say he worked there in 1957-58, and he told me to call Dave Lyle, who confirmed that there was a government office on the corner of Margaret & Johnston, with John Strom's grocery store, then West Coast Cleaners, which are apparent in the picture above, loaned to me by Dick Hawksworth, who said the last name of the owner was "Turone" in 1948. Does anyone know if that was the original owner of the cleaners?

The building to the left of West Coast Cleaners is a business I have yet to identify(please let me know if you know) A little further down the street you can see where Dolan's Sand & Gravel was located.(the dance studio and Rob Price's barbershop are on that site today) Dick says the picture was taken from the roof of the Arlington Hotel in 1944 or '45. The building on the left was Hunt's Meat Market. Dick has also provided this 60 year old picture of what one would have seen looking up Johnston. You'll notice Chatwin Motors was the Ford Dealer, and next door was the future location of C & M Collision. You may be able to spot the two sailors on the extreme right, which leads Dick to believe this photo was also taken in early 1945. More on this in coming weeks.

Another Familiar Face..

Remember Don Gunn from the Lantern Inn?? Don and his three partners John Lee, Len Gunn and John Mah, opened the legendary eatery on Beaver Creek Road, next to the Gill School (where Arbutus RV will be opening soon) in November, 1959. A fire in August of that year, destroyed the original Lantern Inn, which had opened July 1, 1956, on lower Third Avenue.

A Page From Lionel Cyr's Scrapbook....

In the early fifties, the CYO (Catholic Youth Organization) had a softball team. In 1950, the sponsor changed to the Alberni Tyee, under which name this team played, being known as "The Alberni Tyees." See how many faces you recognize in the photo below:::

Back row, left to right::Joe Molly, Ed Davies, John Steigman, Lionel Houle, Raoul Gaudreault, Gary Katrichak, Raymond Sevigny. Front row, left to right::Lionel Cyr, Mike Kwalchuck, Frank Piggon, Al Grant, Omer Blais, Victor Kropniniski, Sammy Hergert.

Missing from the picture are Casnille Cyr and Jerry Cain. Lionel Houle was the president and coach. Lionel Cyr being underage to play(15 years old) was signed in by Lionel Houle.

Another point of interest is that Raoul Gaudreault was always playing without the use of a glove. The teams to beat in 1950 were the Alberni Merchants and Camp One.

This Was Then...
Remembers Old Ike

HEATHER THOMSON PENNYWORTH

For many years now the name Ike Patterson has been synonymous with the Pennyworth.

Every week people picked up the paper and flipped excitedly to his pages to see what new photo or tidbit he had dug up for that week's column. Through his pages people were given a chance to remember, reminisce and even have a laugh at the past.

It was his gift to the community. Now that "Old Ike" won't be around to share those special moments, it comes down to us to carry on a tradition he started. Because people loved his pages so much, we will continue them. Ike completed two pages of his This was Then feature before his death, and so this week we are running them in his memory.

In the future, it will take on a slightly different look as someone else puts his or her own personal flare to the history feature in the Pennyworth. But his love and passion for history will always remain a part of this paper.

Since Ike's death on Sunday, we have received many condolences and heard lots of tales about his past and how he touched different members of the community with his stories and photos. Now we want to invite you to share your favourite Ike story.

For years, he reminded you of your past and the history of the Alberni Valley, now it's your turn.

Send us your photos, stories and favourite memory of Ike.

We will then share them with readers in next week's Pennyworth. It will be our final tribute to Ike and his passion for preserving and enjoying the history of this community and the people who live here.

We hope you enjoy this week's This was Then feature, and we look forward to receiving your memories so we can share them with the rest of Ike's readers.

Please send your submissions to info@thepennyworth.ca, by noon on May 9.

IKE PATTERSON 1947 - 2011

It is with great sadness that we announce the sudden passing of Ike Patterson.

Ike passed unexpectedly at his home. He is predeceased by the love of his life Linda and granddaughter Ella.

He is survived by his three children Tara (Steve), Kris and Arron (Michelle) and eight grandchildren.

Ike has been an influential member of the community since he moved to the area in 1967. He met his wife, Linda Patterson in 1969, and they were married in 1972.

'Old Ike' started working at the local radio station in 1967, where he stayed until 1995. Ike then branched out and started his popular 'Our Town' and 'This was Then' features in the *Pennyworth*.

Ike has served his community as a city councillor since 2002.

He was also fascinated with the history of the Alberni Valley, and was a regular at the museum. He also was a member of the Centennial Committee, a Celebration of Port Alberni and Alberni's 100th Anniversary.

A public service will take place on Friday, May 6, 2011, at the Alberni Valley United Church (3747 Church St.) at 1 p.m.

Ike Patterson and Alberni Valley Museum director Jean McIntosh unwraps the Two Spot plaque for the first time since it returned to the Alberni Valley. The plaque was removed from the No. 7 train sometime around 1979. Ike covered a bit of its history in the Pennyworth Dec. 16, 2010.

www.ingramcontent.com/pod-product-compliance
Lightning Source LLC
Chambersburg PA
CBHW081136170426
43197CB00017B/2874